The Little Book of
FINANCIAL WISDOM

Garth Turner

KEY PORTER BOOKS

Copyright © 2001 by Garth Turner

All rights reserved. No part of this work covered by the copyrights hereon may be reproduced or used in any form or by any means—graphic, electronic or mechanical, including photocopying, recording, taping or information storage and retrieval systems—without the prior written permission of the publisher, or in the case of photocopying or other reprographic copying, a license from the Canadian Copyright Licensing Agency.

National Library of Canada Cataloguing in Publication Data

Turner, Garth
    The little book of financial wisdom

Includes index.
ISBN 1-55263-371-3

1. Finance, Personal – Canada. 2. Financial security. I. Title.

HG179.T873 2002   332.024'01'0971   C2001-901680-8

The publisher gratefully acknowledges the support of the Canada Council for the Arts and the Ontario Arts Council for its publishing program.

We acknowledge the financial support of the Government of Canada through the Book Publishing Industry Development Program (BPIDP) for our publishing activities.

Key Porter Books Limited
70 The Esplanade
Toronto, Ontario
Canada M5E 1R2

www.keyporter.com

Design: Peter Maher
Electronic formatting: Jean Lightfoot Peters

Printed and bound in Canada

01 02 03 04 05 6 5 4 3 2 1

Contents

Do you have five minutes?   5

Your investing style   8

September 11   12

The truth about the stock market   16

The future is technology   20

The Long Wave   24

Can you live without gold?   28

The case for real estate   32

The case against real estate   36

The right real estate strategy   40

Living in volatile times   44

Why you should have RRSPs   49

Why RRSPs can be a terrible idea   53

Buy the Boom   56

The Next Big Thing   60

Inflation and deflation   64

The myth of risk   68

Should you be insured?   71

Other people's money   76

Children   80

Roadkill on Bay Street   83

Diversify, diversify, diversify   86
The lessons of Nortel   90
How to be a market winner   94
Make that mortgage tax-deductible   98
Is there such a thing as good debt?   101
The only way to earn money   105
The burden of wealth   108
Don't beat the Street   112
Dollarization   116
How to find an adviser you can trust   120
garth.ca   124
Index   126

Do you have five minutes?

Sure you do. We all do. Five minutes to take a shower, have a smoke, walk the dog, eat lunch, send an e-mail, get dressed, prepare President's Choice or make love. It's amazing what we fit into five minutes now that our lives are so busy, complex and changeable. Time has turned into a luxury most of us do not have. This is a book that respects that fact.

While time is short, however, the need to understand what's going on around us, especially with our money and our financial futures, has never been greater. As the World Trade Center attacks showed us, everything can change in a single defining day. In the last couple of years we have seen stock markets hit their highest points ever, only to plunge without warning. We're in an age of stunning technological advance, and yet every RRSP with tech stocks in it has been nailed. And speaking of retirement, changes in tax laws may actually have turned your RRSP into a bad idea.

Today it seems that we live in a volatile and explosive age, when mortgage rates and taxes are coming down yet it's actually harder to get ahead. But where do you find the time to learn what the best mutual funds are, how to make your mortgage tax-deductible, or what kind of insurance or real estate to buy? In an uncertain world where terrorism lives, should you have a little gold? Would you be in trouble if the government decided to adopt the American dollar? Should you buy bonds or stocks—and which ones? How do you find an adviser you can trust? Do you even need one? Will Nortel come back? Should you borrow money to invest, and can you easily and legally slash your tax bill?

This book is designed to give you the answer to just about all of these questions in five-minute increments. That's the average time it will take you to read each column I have written. Read one on the subway, or during your next break. Read six over the lunch hour and still have time to get some fresh air. Turn off the TV after dinner and read the whole book.

I know some people have written entire books on many of the topics these columns explore. In fact, count me among them. My books have covered investing in mutual funds and stocks, buying and selling real estate, demographics and the economy, and tax and investment strategies. Over the last few years I've given hundreds of financial seminars in just about every town and city in Canada. My company, Millennium Media Television, has produced more than four hundred programs on personal finance for network TV. I've had a lot of experience being an entrepreneur, creating wealth and jobs, and dealing with risk, sometimes intense, frightening and uncontrollable.

In my own life I've made distinct choices about where to invest, and for how long; how much money to put into a piece of real estate; whether to buy or lease my car; how to insure myself and prepare for the future; how to achieve personal financial and employment independence; and how to find financial peace. I learned some tough lessons in public life, from the sting of a political defeat to the unfettered vitriol of media critics who think my ideas are dangerous. I've been a journalist, author, lecturer, politician, broadcaster, entrepreneur and iconoclast. My beliefs were forged in the real world, doing real things: Sitting at the Cabinet table in Ottawa. Interviewing men and women who move millions of dollars a day. Working the floor of the stock exchange. Creating companies and making payroll. Buying and selling land and houses. Travelling to more corners of this country than some prime ministers have seen, talking to tens of thousands of people a year.

So, I've seen a great deal—what works, and what does not. I've learned that most people do not have the time in their lives to be researching and investigating every decision and financial move they must make. As a consequence many of them have failed, or are heading towards failure. They misinterpret the economy, make the wrong investments, pay too much tax, borrow the wrong way, buy the wrong house, pick the wrong adviser and listen to the wrong sources.

The average Canadian right now is woefully unprepared for a retirement that could last thirty or forty years, especially if that Canadian is a woman. Most of us pay far more tax than need be. We live in the wrong place. We have bad insurance, and routinely buy stocks and mutual funds after they have peaked. These are conditions I see every day, and it's no surprise. We are all busy making a living, raising children, trying to stay healthy and on track. But to achieve financial peace, most people need to know more.

Ironically, it's my belief that we are in the early stages of a financial renaissance that will bring some huge opportunities to prosper, grow wealth rapidly and achieve personal financial freedom—just in time for those who have yet to find the right path. But the time to act is now, to change quickly what needs correcting and make the right, positive moves.

The need to understand the world around us—changeable, exciting, awe-inspiring, sometimes horrifying—has never been greater. Only with informed and up-to-date opinion can we know how to react to events—like those of September 2001—that overwhelm us, engendering fear and quite often the urge to take immediate action. Most people lack this. Their actions are the wrong ones. But those who have knowledge and balance can survive, and prosper, no matter what the news of the day turns out to be.

Do you have five minutes?

Venus descending

Want to boost your odds of outliving your money? Then follow this advice for women put forth by a major bank under the heading, "If you're from Venus, then why get your financial advice from Mars?"
- "Establish a cash reserve of three to six months' worth of living expenses."
- "Don't spend more than 35% of your income to pay off debt (including mortgage and rent)."

- "Get adequate life insurance—eight to ten times your annual family income."

Let's hope Venus finds a rich guy to marry, because she's going to need the dough after following those loser strategies. The goal is to build wealth, not just to conserve what you've got. Here's what Mars suggests:

- Don't have money sitting around earning almost nothing. Invest everything and use a personal line of credit for emergencies.
- Spend as much as you want on debt if it's the right kind: tax-deductible debt used for investment.
- Forget life insurance until you have a reason to buy it. When you do, invest in a product, like universal life, that can also give you tax-sheltered income and growth.

Your investing style

A great deal of this book deals with risk and reward. History shows us that those who take the greatest risk usually reap the greatest reward, but must live with the constant threat of loss.

Readers will find that several of my strategies involve more risk than average Canadians will ever accept. Since no one path is right for all of us, I urge you to stop now and complete the following questionnaires. The first will let you gauge your tolerance for risk. The second will provide you with a snapshot of your own success. The more your net worth needs improving, the greater the risk you should shoulder. In fact, the real risk for most of us is not losing our money, but outliving it.

Risk test

Until you know your risk profile, it's impossible to set realistic goals and then select the investment assets that will achieve them. There are many risk analyzers around, such as Bank of Montreal's "MatchMaker," which you can access on the Internet (www.bmo.com/mutualfunds/ps/matchmaker_test). Most financial advisory outfits, like RBC Capital Markets or

ScotiaMcLeod, also have extensive surveys intended to assess your tolerance for risk. But I like the one below, despite its American origin, because it's so simple. Give it a try.

Instructions: Here is a series of statements designed to help you decide how you feel about investment risk. Which one sounds more like you, the one on the left or the one on the right? Or are you somewhere in the middle? For each pair of statements, put a check mark beside the number that best indicates where you fall between the two statements.

My primary goal is to protect my savings. I am most concerned about losing what I have, and am not willing to take any risk just to keep up with inflation.	1. __ 2. __ 3. __ 4. __ 5. __	My primary goal is to earn enough on my savings to stay ahead of inflation. I am willing to take on some investment risk to do so.
I would worry about short-term investment losses, even if I didn't need my retirement savings for twenty years.	1. __ 2. __ 3. __ 4. __ 5. __	I wouldn't worry about short-term investment losses, as long as I didn't need my savings in the near future.
If the stock market dropped 500 points tomorrow, I'd probably take my losses and pull my savings out of stocks to keep from losing more money.	1. __ 2. __ 3. __ 4. __ 5. __	If the stock market dropped 500 points tomorrow, I'd probably put more of my money into the market to catch it before it moves back up.
I would definitely be upset if my investment statement showed a loss.	1. __ 2. __ 3. __ 4. __ 5. __	A loss on my investment statement wouldn't necessarily bother me.
If I had a choice between $1,000 cash and a 1-in-10 chance at $10,000, I'd definitely take the cash.	1. __ 2. __ 3. __ 4. __ 5. __	If I had a choice between $1,000 cash and a 1-in-10 chance at $10,000, I'd definitely take the chance.

| I wouldn't invest in a start-up company, even one with a promising idea. The risk of losing the entire investment is just too great. | 1. __ 2. __ 3. __ 4. __ 5. __ | I'd invest in a start-up company if it had a promising idea. I have to take some chances to earn a really good return. |

Answer Score

6–10 Very Conservative; 11–15 Conservative; 16–20 Moderate; 21–30 Aggressive.

Source: First Union Bank

Net worth worksheet

Make a copy of this and complete it once a year, on your birthday. The goal, obviously, is to have a growing net worth, as well as a steady shift of your wealth from real assets (such as vehicles and real estate) to financial assets (like mutual funds and bonds).

Assets		**Market Value**
Real assets:		
Real estate	Principal residence	
	Cottage	
	Other	
Vehicles	Primary	
	Collector	
	Other (aircraft etc.)	
Furniture	Household	
	Antique	
Precious metals	Gold, silver	
Collectibles	Art, etc.	
Equipment	Tools	
	Farm equipment	
Other real assets		
	TOTAL	
Financial assets:		
Bank accounts	Savings	
	Chequing	
Term deposits, GICs		
Savings bonds		
RRSPs		

RRIFS
Government/corporate bonds
Mutual funds
Segregated funds
Stocks
Life insurance policies (cash value)
Other marketable securities
Mortgages receivable
Business interests (shareholder's equity)
                              TOTAL

TOTAL ASSETS

Real assets:
This year _____ % Last year _____ %
Financial assets
This year _____ % Last year _____ %

Liabilities		**Outstanding balance**
Mortgage	Principal residence	_____
	Cottage	_____
	Investment property	_____
Line of credit		_____
Credit cards		_____
Personal loans		_____
Margin accounts		_____
Shareholder's loans		_____
Accounts payable		_____
Other liabilities		_____
	TOTAL	_____

NET WORTH (assets minus liabilities) _____

Last year   _____
Gain (loss)   _____ (_____)

September 11

In the months following the September 11 terrorists attacks on New York and Washington, the fear of physical danger was replaced, and surpassed, by the fear that everything had changed. The raging bull stock market was dead. The Canadian ability to ignore Americans was gone forever. The border, for a time, turned into a wall. The neglect of personal security and all things military was proven to have been utterly wrong. The promise of peaceful globalization was replaced by the reality that a few madmen could turn a commercial jetliner into a flying bomb—anywhere, anytime—thanks to the very openness that global trade had wrought.

Mostly, we feared that war was upon us. Capitalism had been attacked in the most blatant fashion possible and the economic implications were immediate and global. More than 100,000 airline workers on four continents were out of work within two weeks. Corporate profits plunged and the Dow had its worst week since the Great Depression. Central bankers scrambled to cut interest rates and pump out new money, but admitted that Nine Eleven would likely mean a recession, although hopefully a short one.

Investors were paralyzed at first, then terrified. Rivers of money flowed from mutual funds that invested in stocks to ones that hid in cash. Sales of corporate bonds, guaranteed investment certificates and savings bonds mushroomed. The price of gold jumped and gold coins were in hot demand. It was a classic response. But was it the right one? Had everything really changed, or had we just forgotten the past?

I did not experience the Second World War or Pearl Harbor, but I do have other memories. In 1955 I was six years old. Each week at school, my teacher insisted that we practice crawling under our desks in case a nuclear strike took place during the day. We all hoped it would happen when we were home, since most families (including mine) maintained and stocked basement bomb shelters.

In October 1962, the Soviets and the Americans played chicken over the installation of nuke-tipped missiles in Cuba. In my neighborhood, air raid sirens were installed and civil defence drills were common.

On the fourth day of May in 1970, my girlfriend (now my wife) and I were catching a ride with my father, taking an afternoon away from university to visit Niagara Falls. On the car radio came news that a number of students at Kent State University, protesting the Vietnam war, had been shot and killed by the National Guard. The American economy was in crisis as the ongoing war drained resources and the U.S. teetered on the brink of bankruptcy.

On October 19, 1987, I was a newspaper columnist and editor in Toronto, watching as the New York Stock Exchange lost 22% of its value in a single day. It was without exception the worst crash in history, ushering in the end of a decade that was marked by runaway inflation, 20% interest rates and $800-an-ounce gold. It looked like the end of capitalism. I headed for the newspaper library to find photos from the Great Depression: I wanted to remind readers of what to expect.

In 1991 I was a Member of Parliament walking into the government lobby of the House of Commons. The prime minister came in and, in a hushed voice, called us over for a briefing. Standing on a table, he told us that Canadian CF-18s had just been ordered to take part in the bombing of Iraq. The Gulf War shot oil prices sky-high and had an entire world glued to nonstop coverage on CNN. The horror was addictive.

September 11, 2001 brought more horror, conflict and uncertainty. The events that were breaking around us had unknown outcomes and continue to play out even today. But if history is any guide—at least from my five decades on this earth—then what is shocking and unnerving today will pass tomorrow. The economy, and the stock market that tracks it, has absorbed all of

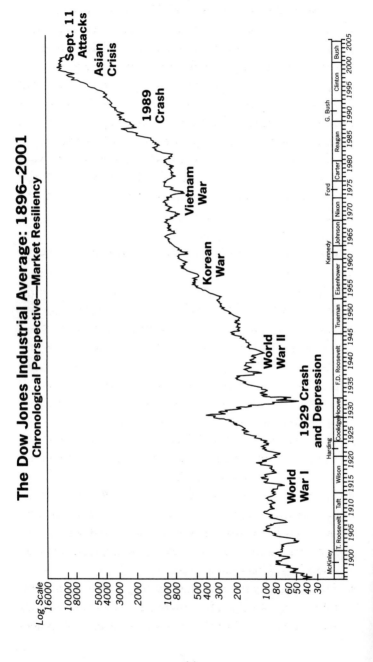

these shocks and eventually moved on. Setbacks like the Cold War, the Vietnam War and the Gulf War evolved into more stable and improved situations. Financial crises like the 1987 Crash, the Asian flu, the Mexican peso collapse and Y2K were all followed by substantial gains and the creation of wealth.

Despite this new brand of war, and the corporate and market carnage it's engendered, things will get better. Stocks will rise. The economy will grow. Technology will advance. Inflation is still in check, interest rates are falling and governments still have lots of cash. There is no reason to turn a paper loss into a real one by bailing out of falling investments. If you did not move to protect your assets before September 11, by 10 a.m. that morning it was too late.

Here is what I believe Nine Eleven will come to mean. This will also explain why I have included some particular themes in this book:

- Harmonization of key national policies—defence, immigration and national Security—with the United States will take place. This follows on the trade and economic integration that began with the Auto Pact and culminated in the Free Trade and NAFTA agreements. September 11, 2001 proved North America can no more be carved up into independent regions than continental airspace.
- This harmonization will lead inevitably to one North American currency, and it will not be the Canadian loonie. Are you ready for dollarization?
- The war on terrorism, led by George W. Bush and his NATO allies, cannot be won. Although our collective security can be improved, terror is now an everyday fact of life in North America, as it is in Palestine. Expect a commensurate loss of personal freedom.
- The uncertainty this will cause makes government stimulus a sure-thing. Watch for lower interest rates and permanently lower taxes in North America. Expect government

surpluses to erode temporarily into deficits as huge amounts are spent on continental defence and tax relief.
- Stock markets have huge upside potential. Not only were equities oversold in the weeks following the attacks, but capitalism survived its greatest assault. Combined with government actions, these elements will fuel a market rally of the kind that followed the 1987 crash. Wise investors will see it early.
- Conversely, residential real estate will become more illiquid as the population age and North Americans realize the best defence against uncertainty is wealth you can quickly get your hands on. Some kinds of real estate will appreciate, many will not. Choose carefully.
- More importantly than ever before, investors need to be diversified, well-informed and unemotional. Shun stocks for mutual funds; ignore hot tips; make your debt deductible; earn income the right way; seek personal advice; and study history, where there is comfort. There have been shocks and danger before. In each, there was opportunity.

The truth about the stock market

If you believe in capitalism, then you must believe in the stock market. Without it, the economies of Canada and the United States would be feudal today. A handful of obscenely wealthy families would control the most powerful corporations, which in turn would rule the workforce and the lives of individuals. New companies, fresh entrepreneurs and good ideas would be denied access to capital, and life as we know it today would simply not exist.

Nowadays, the stock market is more powerful than religion or the government, as should be the case. It knows no one master, reacts to no single influence and is moved by every human emotion, including greed, fear, lust, worry, ambition and irrational exuberance. It is both predictable and unpredictable, volatile and stable, the creator and destroyer of wealth. It could be man's finest invention.

Two thousand years ago, investors traded securities on the streets of Rome. Stocks were first swapped in Antwerp in 1500. London's first exchange came in 1773, Philadelphia's in 1790 and Toronto's in 1878. The Dow Jones index was created in 1889 and the TSE 300 in 1977. Computers came to Bay Street that same year, and eventually the trading floor was closed and everything went digital.

Today, Stock Market Place in the Exchange Tower on Toronto's King Street is a museum, populated only by school tours, media outlets looking for a business backdrop, and a handful of former floor traders who give presentations on how things used to be. Above and surrounding them are office towers holding vast brokerage company trading floors, brimming with computers and containing adrenalin-whipped young men and women who move billions of dollars as so many blips on their screens.

Universally, the Canadian media portrays the market as a casino. We are told it represents risk. Stock market advances are reported in the business section; stock market crashes are kept for the front page. Between 1995 and 2001 the Toronto stock market doubled in value, giving diversified, long-term investors an annual return of almost 20%. But the big stories for reporters on Bay Street were the Asian flu of 1998, the Y2K crisis of 1999, the dot-com tech wreck of 2000, the Nortel implosion of 2001 and the terrorist attacks, on New York and Washington.

The myth about the stock market is articulated every day in your newspaper and on your television set and car radio. The truth about the market is that it is the single best, most secure and profitable place to put your wealth, so long as you do it properly in both a physical and spiritual fashion. History has proven that equities have over time consistently outperformed all other kinds of assets. The reason is simple: the market paces and reflects economic growth, and the story of mankind is the story of advance, innovation and achievement. Since the Second World War the rate of ascent has been giddy.

In 1945 people bought ice blocks for their refrigerators, and telephones were unusual. Most rural areas had not been electrified, and there were no television channels. No Internet. No fax. No computers. No calculators. No air conditioners. No seat belts. No dishwashers. No transistors or chips. No birth control pill, DNA mapping or heart surgery. Life expectancy was fifty-one and the world was lurching from its greatest war to four decades of arms buildup and the brink of nuclear obliteration.

One generation ago, most people had nothing to do with the stock market. Today it is completely accessible, democratized, and an influence on the lives of everyone who uses money. Over the past half-century the market has been central to the explosive growth of the economy, and it has reflected it at the same time. There was no risk for anyone who invested in that market over the long haul, only for those who put money in, then withdrew it at the wrong time, such as during the bear market of the 1970s or following the crash of 1987.

This will be the same pattern going forward. Expect more unbridled growth in North America as the Internet becomes the umbilical cord that eventually binds every home to every other, develops into the dominant channel of communication, information and entertainment in every car, bus, truck, tractor, plane, corporation, purse and pocket. Expect decades of expansion as biotechnology extends life to untested limits and brings about the regeneration of human organs themselves. Cancer, Alzheimer disease, heart disease, diabetes—all the ailments and afflictions of old age and premature death—will be gone within the lifetime of today's children. Borders and national currencies will erode in the face of globalization and free trade. After five thousand years of human history we will finally be freed of the destructive forces of tribalism that were the root causes of mistrust and war. The terrorist bombings that rocked the U.S. in the autumn of 2001 represented a desperate attempt by those who believe in closed societies to stop the spread of North American–style capitalism. And while their actions temporarily disrupted stock market trading, and caused some turbulence in the markets, their ultimate goal failed.

A coming Utopia, certainly not. But it's hard not to believe that the twin forces of technology and biotechnology will reshape our entire society within the next two decades. My father's eighty-five years extended from a time when stagecoaches rumbled through southern Ontario to the moment a Canadian walked in space. Will my life see any less revolution? Of course not, and that is why there is no risk in a stock market that is, in effect, an index of ongoing human achievement and a marker of its temporary failures.

The risk and danger that the media underscores come only when investors believe they know more than the market does; when they buy for greed or sell out of fear. Then they deserve what the market delivers, as do those who know how, and when, to embrace it.

Buy high, sell low

In the last stock market bubble—the technology and dot-com circus of 1999–2000—lots of people became "investors" who were actually market timers. They jumped on the roller-coaster car when it was already at the top of the loop. They jumped off when it was at the bottom. "Buy high and sell low" should be on our national coat of arms. When it comes to the stock market:
- Don't buy anything unless you plan to own it for at least five years. Time dilutes risk.
- Know your tolerance for risk, because it's probably a whole lot lower than you think it is. Take the risk test on pages 8–10.
- Mitigate risk by diversifying your investments. Don't buy Nortel but a

science and technology fund that has lots of companies in it. Better still, invest in an equity fund that gives you exposure to lots of sectors.
- Never pick stocks or mutual funds based on media stories. Conrad Black wouldn't.

The future is technology

The window on human achievement is art. The engine of it is technology, and that is poised to accelerate as never before. The stunning advances of the last fifty years have turned the planet from a tribal place into a global one. New technologies—radio, television, satellite communications and the Internet—disallow national propaganda and regional thought.

In the future, technology will let humanity take the next steps, and they will be nothing short of extreme. The Internet will become the central nervous system of the world. Personal computers will approximate human thought and fit into your pocket. Biotechnology could allow the production of meat without the raising of animals, and the manufacture of pharmaceuticals from grass and water. Space technology could deliver non-polluting energy to the globe. Nanotechnology could prolong human life by modifying genetic structures. Information technology could forever wipe away poverty and regional disparities through e-commerce.

Already we can see the seeds of these events. The Internet is the fastest-spreading technology in the history of the world, growing at a rate three times faster than that experienced by television and 700% faster than the spread of electricity. In 2001, 51% of Canadian households had at least one person using the Internet, while virtually 100% of schools were on-line. The cost of doing business and running governments is falling exponentially as new applications are found. Sending business proposals, transferring text and video files, replacing air travel with teleconferencing, e-filing taxes, getting passport applications on-line, and monitoring your kids at daycare via streaming video are becoming routine, enabling a giant boost in productivity that will be at the core of explosive future economic growth.

Despite the tech wreck of 2000–2001 that burned off 90% or more from the value of some technology, dot-com and Internet companies, this is clearly the future. In fact the market meltdown has set the stage for healthier, more robust and more focused growth going forward. Investors will be looking for serious and practical applications of technology at every stage to ensure a positive cash flow, which will in turn allow the discovery and deployment of the next application. The historic pattern of investing in technologies has been repeated: as with the railroads at the end of the nineteenth century and the automobile at the dawn of the twentieth, so has this century begun with an irrational overenthusiasm for a new technology that created an unsustainable bubble.

Now that the bubble has been burst, rational application of that technology can take place, amid one of the most favourable investment climates in history for those with the vision to see what, clearly, is coming. Consider some of these conclusions, drawn from sources as varied as IBM, PricewaterhouseCoopers and the United Nations Millennium Project:

- Personal computers, today capable of about a billion operations a second, will, within twenty years, perform a *million billion* operations in the same time. That will take the computing power from the level of a lizard brain to that of a human brain. Most of the computing power will be in handheld devices, like mobile phones.

    A next step is pervasive or ubiquitous computing, as everyday devices—washing machines, televisions, cars and home security systems—become smart and interconnected; are able to register faults, fit into a wider pattern of usage, and relate to each other; and are always on-line. The infrastructure to make this possible is already in place: the global fibre-optics system that Lucent, Nortel, 360networks and JDS Uniphase rushed to build just slightly before the data existed to fill the pipes.

- In space, commercialization of flights and visits to the international space station will fund the rapid deployment of useful applications like solar-powered satellites with the capability to deliver energy without generating any waste, and instant, universal communications among fixed and mobile users. Already, cars are being produced with always-on satellite global positioning systems connected to built-in cellular phones. The next step is Internet connectivity, which is imminent. The space race of the 1960s and 1970s has yielded to a massive international collaborative effort that will hasten the industrialization of the earth's orbit. The cost of space technology will plunge as dramatically as the cost of a personal computer did in the 1990s.

- In terms of biotechnology, this will become the "Biological Century." As Jerome Glenn and Theodore Gordon wrote in their 2000 UN paper:

"Gene technology and clone technology can create new biological species, decrease the starvation of the globe, and improve the condition of the developing nations... biotechnology in animal husbandry will also provide animals that serve as production facilities for human pharmaceuticals. Cows will be seen as bio-reactors, making valuable products. The human gene for insulin or clotting factor, for example, can be inserted into the germ plasma of cattle and sheep at a genetic location that leads to easy harvesting of the desired human chemical in urine, blood or milk. Cloning these animals then makes available large quantities of drugs that today may be more valuable than platinum or gold. Feed the cow hay and water, and get pharmaceuticals.

"Transgenic crops will transform marginal agricultural

areas—deserts or industrial lands—into prolific breadbaskets. Genetic medicines will cure diseases from the inside, whereas today's intrusive medicine works from the outside. Human cloning technology holds out the serious promise of the production of organs from your own genetic material. Umbilical cord cells are routinely being stored today for the future manufacture of spare body parts. And stem cells from cattle or fish could be used to grow muscle tissue in production facilities, precluding the necessity of raising and slaughtering entire animals for food. Foot-and-mouth or mad cow disease would be a thing of the distant germ- and virus-laden past."

- Nanotechnology is the microminiaturization of existing technologies, seen by U.S. scientist Neal Lane as the "most likely area of science and engineering to produce the breakthroughs of tomorrow." Included could be nanotubes that allow for miniature electronics and the manufacture at home of devices like computers.
- Information technology is exploding now as never before, and it holds infinite potential to create humanity's most important communication tool ever, far more powerful than the book, the telephone or television, because it will absorb and modify everything.

One-way media will be replaced entirely by interactive media. Newspapers will disappear, as will conventional television and radio. Streaming video, voice, text and video e-mail, and radio will be seamless pieces of the communications pipe all of us are a part of. Internet access will become a right of national citizenship, because without it citizens will not have access to education, services or even the electoral process.

None of these applications of new technology is implausible. Nor are they far distant. They all herald a new chapter in the human story, where war, struggle, darkness, disease and division can be swept away. Technology is the future, more spectacularly than ever before. Investors who understand that, who embrace it amid the rubble of the recent tech meltdown, will never look back.

Show me the money

> If technology is so great, why have trillions of dollars been erased from the investment portfolios of investors who ponied up their cash to buy in?
> - The biggest mistake tech investors make is trying to time the market. Forget it. By the time you hear about a hot stock, it has usually started to flame out. Much better to chase technology through a science and tech mutual fund and let a professional manager find tomorrow's winners.
> - Don't invest in companies that don't make money. Too many people either never bother looking at a company's bottom line or they believe in that great myth of "future profits." *Show me the money.*
> - Make sure any technology investment is in a company that has practical applications. If it can cure a disease, allows other companies to make more money or creates a service people actually want to use, then it has legs.

The Long Wave

One of the benefits of getting older is understanding that everything is not happening for the first time. When it comes to money, investments and the economy, there are cycles. Economies grow rapidly for a while and people gain confidence, so they buy a lot of stuff, putting pressure on prices, leading to inflation and higher interest rates, which make buying things and doing business harder, which leads to lower economic growth and sometimes even recession, which brings deflation and lower rates, setting the scene for economic expansion.

Have you ever wondered why the 1980s, with that decade's

runaway inflation, 22% mortgages, real estate boom and $800-an-ounce gold ended with the October 1987 stock market crash? You should. It's all connected. In fact everything is connected in cycles that are so long, most people find it impossible to see them, or understand where their own lives intersect the curve.

I'm a believer in the Long Wave theory, also known sometimes as the Kondratieff Wave. It was first proposed by a Russian economist, Nikolai Kondratieff (or Kondratyev), in the 1920s. He studied wages and commodity prices (wood, iron, grains, coal) between 1800 and 1900 and concluded that long cycles of between forty-eight and fifty-five years were clearly in evidence.

This theory also supports the following observations about "upwave" periods:

- Long waves are always fuelled by new technologies.
- These technologies spread rapidly.
- There is job loss and disruption as the wave moves higher.
- New companies using new technologies are excessively valued at first.
- Markets are intensely volatile during the process.

Those conditions are familiar to us in the first few years of the twenty-first century. We are in the midst of a technological revolution probably more profound and far-reaching than any that's gone before. The Internet has become the fastest-spreading global technology in history. To reach 30% of the population of North America took just seven years, compared with twenty-six for television and almost fifty for electricity. Certainly there is turmoil in the corporate world as large companies merge, restructure or disappear, and the dot-com bubble proved conclusively that new-technology outfits can be wildly overvalued by investors. (That has certainly happened before, with railway companies in the late 1800s and radio stocks in the

1920s.) Finally, volatility has become the hallmark of our age, as stock markets routinely move higher or lower by up to a thousand points in a single day.

Are we in an upwave now? Of course, and it could last—if Kondratieff's theory holds—for between fifteen and twenty years, peaking about 2020, just as the Baby Boom generation is turning seventy and becomes a greater financial and medical drag on society than any experienced before.

Take a look at a chart of stock market activity over the last hundred years and match it to the Kondratieff cycle. You will see that the wave was moving higher as the twentieth century began (coming off a recession in the 1880s) and peaked about 1929, the time of the stock market crash. The wave then plunged through the Great Depression years to a Second World War low, before moving higher again through the 1950s and the inflation-ridden 1970s. It peaked in the early eighties, then spiralled lower through the 1987 market crash, before beginning the third upwave in the early 1990s. Today it is showing a jagged-tooth pattern, which, if history repeats, could lead to a rapid movement up through the next decade, perhaps peaking again in the 2020s.

What is fuelling the upwave we are riding today?

A heady mix of powerful influences that too many investors lose sight of in the swirl of daily events and in a world where information overkill can confuse and confound. Among these influences is little or no inflation, which has led to a meaningful decline in the cost of money. Low rates are positive for stocks and boost everyone's purchasing power. At the same time, governments have been able to bring their costs under control for the first time in a generation. Both Canada and the U.S. are in budget surplus, having eliminated their operating deficits, and are in a position to actually pay down debt. They're also able to reverse an eighty-year trend of rising taxation, putting more money into the hands of consumers and investors, promising sustained economic growth.

Trade barriers are falling around the world, leading to a more efficient pattern of manufacturing and consuming. It no longer makes sense to be stamping out hubcaps in a high-wage, high-value-added place like Canada, so those jobs have migrated to low-wage, low-value-added parts of the world. This process has led to job loss and disruption, but it is also the basis for a jump in overall global wealth.

Technology, of course, is boosting productivity in a historic way. The laptop I'm writing this book on can process the words, add graphics and pictures, check spelling and grammar, translate this text into another language, and publish it on the Internet. New technology is creating new opportunities daily, even as it imperils industries that resist innovation and modernization. Volatility, change and progress.

There is also the reality of demographics, as this Baby Boom generation amasses more wealth than any in the past. For the first time, one of the fastest-growing areas of banking is wealth management, as the number of families in Canada with between $250,000 and $1 million to invest doubles by 2010. This torrent of money will fuel the stock market and other financial assets. There is every reason to believe that the Dow Jones Industrials, at the 10,000 mark in 2001, could achieve 20,000 before the end of the decade and 40,000 five years after that. Before you dismiss that prediction, bear in mind that it represents a substantial slowing in the market's growth compared with the last fifteen years—a period that gave us the 1987 crash, double-digit interest rates, the Gulf War, Y2K, near impeachment of the U.S. president, the destabilization of Russia, the Asian flu, the technology bubble and its burst, and soaring energy costs.

The spark plugs of the upwave will surely be biotechnology, the Internet and wireless applications, layered over the longest period of global peace and prosperity in human history, at least for the next fifteen years or so—years to build wealth for what comes after.

Road map to independence

Do you know your net worth? Most people don't, and without that key piece of information it's impossible to plot a road map to financial independence. Use the **Net Worth worksheet** on pages 10–11 to obtain this crucial snapshot of where you are, and then repeat the exercise annually. Here are some things to look for:

- If your liabilities exceed your assets, then the first action to take is to find ways of paying down your debt, especially debt with an obscene interest rate attached to it, such as credit card balances. Consider the wisdom of a home equity loan to consolidate high-rate debts.
- If the bulk of your net worth is tied up in your house, as is the case with most people, then it's time to diversify. Assets like bonds, preferred shares or royalty trusts can pay you regular and predictable income. Others, like equities, have consistently outperformed real estate. And given the twin dangers of deflation (as opposed to inflation) and demographics (an aging population), real estate values are as likely to fall in the years to come as to rise.

Can you live without gold?

In times of war, uncertainty, upheaval, prosperity and inflation—for the four thousand years preceding our lives today—humans coveted gold. It was always considered a form of money, since it is portable, instantly recognizable, durable, divisible and virtually indestructible. For most of civilized history, right up to the 1970s, gold was at the very foundation and heart of the international monetary system. Our paper money once carried words saying that the bearer would be paid upon demand in bullion. But with the end of the gold standard under the Bretton Woods agreement in 1971, all that changed. Today there is hardly any gold standing behind the value of Canadian dollars; rather, our currency is backed by the government's ability to tax.

Before the 1970s, a Canadian dollar was worth a dollar. Today, on a good day, it's worth sixty-six U.S. pennies. In fact the American dollar has emerged as the new global currency, and a greenback that is currently overvalued has decimated other currencies around the world. The standard of the monetary system is no longer a physical, rare, beautiful, historic commodity, but a battery of printing presses in Washington and faith in what 300 million Americans will do next.

So, did we blow it? Is there a case for saying that, in a world undergoing massive structural change, gold is actually the real currency in waiting?

Maybe. So far, since time began, we have refined 142,600 tons of gold. It all still exists. Half is in jewellery, 10% has been used in manufacturing, 20% is still in government reserves, and the rest, about 18%, is in the hands of investors. Because gold has come to be valued in U.S. dollars, and because those dollars are artificially high in value, the price of gold has been artificially depressed. That means it is harder for gold companies to make any money mining new gold.

As a result, gold production is now lagging behind demand. Jewellery manufacturing alone has risen by 45% in the last decade, according to the TD Bank, shooting gold demand higher each year by 2.6%. But in 2000, only 2,573 tons of new gold were mined, less than the 3,946 tons that were bought for jewellery, industrial uses or hoarding. How can the price of a commodity be static or declining when demand is rising?

That is the fault of governments, and governments alone.

For the last twenty-five years, governments and official agencies have flooded the market by dumping the gold reserves they carefully built up over decades. The U.S. sold more than 500 tons in the 1970s. The International Monetary Fund disposed of three times that amount between 1976 and 1980. The Bank of Canada over the last twenty years has sold an astonishing 653 tons of bullion. In 1965 we owned well over 1,000 tons; today we own 37. Other sellers since 1987 include Britain,

Belgium, Austria, Switzerland and Argentina. In all, governments have got rid of 3,600 tons of gold.

Then there is another official practice that has hurt the metal: central bank gold lending. These national, government-controlled banks have routinely lent gold reserves to private gold bullion banks at very low lease rates. The bullion banks sell the gold in the spot market, invest the money in fixed assets paying more than it costs them to lease the gold, and then promise to buy new gold in the future at a fixed rate from mining companies.

As a result, gold that has yet to be mined is brought to market through hedging, which increases supply and depresses prices, and this procedure is essentially financed by government reserves. Over the last ten years the amount of government gold lent out has increased more than 270%. This practice, however, could be curtailed over the next half-decade as a result of a multi-government agreement signed in 1999.

Still, the argument is a strong one that the very governments which have opted to back their currencies with nothing but their own economies have played a pivotal role in destroying the intrinsic value of gold. And there is fear and concern among some people that the entire world has hitched its wagon, dangerously, to the Americans.

Gold prices have now been in a volatile free fall for twenty years. The last serious gold rush took place in 1980, when fears of runaway inflation and a meltdown in the value of the greenback had people lining up to buy an ounce for $850 U.S. I remember seeing people waiting in a queue in downtown Toronto that stretched down two city blocks outside a trust company that handed over gold bars and wafers from the wickets inside.

Ten years later, inflation was still a concern, but the gold market had been flooded with government bullion, and the price of an ounce had fallen to $400 U.S. The downward trend continued, with bullion entering the new millennium at just $270. More recently, in the aftermath of the September 11 attacks, gold spiked briefly as panic swept the globe.

Economists at the Toronto Dominion Bank believe the overvalued American dollar will decline over the next couple of years, as global demand for gold continues to rise thanks to a steady rebound in the world economy. The result will be $320-an-ounce gold by 2002. But it could be much higher, since rising gold prices do not translate instantly into rising production.

In fact, gold could explode.

Paper money is coming to the end of its time as a useful, practical commodity. It is being replaced by digital wealth in the form of credit, debit and stored-value cards for everyday use, and electronic funds for investment. We all now go to work and earn money that we never see. It is deposited directly into a bank account, where it is represented on a computer screen, and then transferred to cover expenditures we never physically make—for a mortgage payment, credit card transaction or RRSP contribution. Our investments are digital. We buy wine and groceries with debit cards, and Internet purchases with credit card numbers.

The entire system that governs your financial life is now a giant leap of faith. The money you use every day and the wealth that you accumulate over your lifetime does not have a physical existence, unless you were to operate only with paper money. Interestingly, it's getting harder and harder to find retailers who will accept a fifty-dollar bill.

Imagine a time when that leap of faith could be questioned. It might be the result of an economic, technological or environmental event that disrupts this digital world—something as simple as a continental power outage, as problematic as the effects of global warming, or as unexpected as a missile attack from a rogue nation. At such a time, would you want to own a form of money that is universally recognized, portable, indestructible and divisible?

I thought so. Gold may not be the greatest long-term investment, but neither is life insurance.

All that glitters

You can own gold in several ways. It depends on why you are buying it. Is it an investment asset that will give you a capital gain, or is it something to exchange for bread in a future world where paper money is solely good for lighting the cooking fire of your hillside encampment? Only in the latter case does it make real sense to own the physical metal, and then you have to worry about where to keep it (if paper money is worthless, then the banks that deal in it will likely be toast, along with access to your safety deposit box). For those days when you do not expect Armageddon, here are some better suggestions:
- Gold certificates that represent physical gold bullion, which the seller keeps safe for you.
- Precious metals mutual funds, which own a variety of assets reflecting the value of gold, silver and strategic and precious metals.
- Shares in gold companies, such as Barrick and Placer Dome. They employ a lot of techniques, such as hedging, that can keep profits coming even when world bullion prices decline.

The case for real estate

I admit to being as afflicted as the next guy. Real estate is a powerful drug. It confers wealth, security, place and position. The very city, neighbourhood or street where we live says something about us to everyone else. We harbour deep geographic prejudices that can be more ingrained and harder to overcome than ones based on race, religion or sexual orientation.

This country was built on real estate, from the granting of land to immigrants in the West to the building of Toronto condos worth $600 a square foot. Real estate has defined families and formed the very basis of their economic survival. Lord Elgin granted my ancestors land in pre-Confederation Canada, where they built a home called Elgin Hall in a hamlet they called Mount Elgin. My brother, Elgin, was a constant reminder of the roots that led directly back into the Upper Canadian soil.

My parents' generation equated renting with transience and home ownership with stability and community involvement. They also installed real estate as the cornerstone of personal financial planning and wealth accumulation, first moving up as the family's needs grew, then just trading houses every few years to cash in on the inevitable capital gains.

I'm guilty too. My passion for historic properties, for acres and acres of forest and river, for the thrill of owning a bucolic vista or windows opening onto the financial core of the country's greatest, teeming city—this has all cost me a lot of money, and it has not always brought a corresponding gain. But I'd do it again. Every property was bought with enthusiasm. Every closing day was a rush, every new key a treasure.

It has never been easier to buy property than it is today. This is the result of many factors, including a government program allowing home ownership with just 5% of the purchase price down and 95% financing. It also results from intense competition among mortgage lenders, which has led to an unprecedented degree of financing flexibility and consistently low mortgage rates.

Perhaps the greatest benefit of owning residential real estate is the tax-free capital gain. This is the only asset you can own that yields a profit totally free of tax, which underscores the most favoured status that society and its government gives to the family home.

Since I have so enjoyed owning real estate all of my adult life, it would be hypocritical of me to criticize others who have also relished being landowners. But we have to realize that the times are changing rapidly, and so are the rules of successful real estate ownership. It's no longer a sure thing to buy a house, wait a few years, and then sell for a profit after living there for free. In fact too many people have lost a substantial amount of money by buying the wrong house in the wrong place at the wrong time. A bungalow in Vancouver, in other words, can be just as dangerous and unpredictable an investment as a fistful of Nortel stock.

So, here are some rules to buy by:

- Don't buy more house than you need, and don't buy without ensuring that it's the right financial decision. This is a lesson most young couples need to learn, since home ownership is still the irrational dream of the newly married, just as it was for their parents before them. Many young people put all of their available resources into a down payment, even cashing in their RRSPs, to buy a home with three more bedrooms than they need and requiring a regular flow of money that will keep them house-rich and cash-poor for a decade. It makes more sense to use a small down payment, get the best possible mortgage (with a cashback feature or discounted rate on a variable term), and make sure the house does not suck in 100% of your disposable income. This is only one aspect of your financial plan, not the whole damn thing.
- Know what you can afford before you go shopping. Step One is getting pre-approved for a mortgage. This is simple, fast and free. Use the Internet to log on to the site of any major lender and fill out the pre-approval form. You will be told in mere minutes how much money you qualify to borrow. Add that to your down payment amount and you know precisely how much house you can buy.

    As a rule of thumb, a house should not cost more than two and a half times your gross earnings, and the mortgage payment, plus realty taxes, should not top 30% of your annual income.
- Buy the worst house on the best street. Forget the upgraded kitchen, new wallpaper and Jacuzzi; all that stuff can be added later. It's the location that matters above all when it comes to real estate. Real estate is immovable. It's ultimately worth what it's worth because of where it is.

    So, always buy the worst house on the best street, not the other way around. Buy in the middle of the block instead of on the corner, for more privacy and less traffic. Buy in an established neighbourhood instead of a subdivision on a former cornfield. Buy into a "demand" area rather than a cheap one; it's in demand for a reason.

Buy where there is access to schools and transit, but not across the street from them. In a condo apartment building, buy a high floor. Buy a street with trees. Don't buy near a gas station or dry cleaners or hospital or fire hall. Buy the biggest lot you can, even if the house is tiny: houses you can fix, land you can't.

- Buy what you can sell later. The day you buy should be the one you start thinking about selling. Canadians live in one house for an average of seven years, so chances are you will own a lot of homes—and each time you change, a buyer has to come along. Also remember that real estate tastes change, and as the population ages, they will change even faster. My guess is that big suburban houses are coming to the end of their shelf life, while bungalows and condos will see much more demand.

Buy what has potential for appreciation, because the next guy is likely to think the same way. Don't buy too many bedrooms, or a lot of outside maintenance, or a place with a swimming pool, because these are all increasingly negatives.

View every real estate decision with as much passion as you would a mutual fund purchase. At the end of the day, it is the size of your bank account, not your backyard, that will matter.

Do you need an agent?

I'm no big fan of do-it-yourself financial action plans, and that goes for buying and selling real estate. You can get into serious trouble trying to save a few dollars, especially when it comes to marketing a property.
- Always use an agent to professionally establish the market value of your home. Pick an asking price that's too high and the property will quickly become stale. You could end up having to lowball the house just to get an offer later. An agent will give you comparables and explain why your house is worth what it's worth.

- Always get the house listed on MLS—the Multiple Listing Service—or its local equivalent, operated by the real estate board. This immediately puts the house in front of gobs of hungry realtors, all with their own lists of potential buyers.
- Are real estate commissions negotiable? Is the sky blue? You have complete flexibility these days to sit down with an agent and bargain what his or her percentage will be. In the bad old days it was 6%. Today, 4% is reasonable.
- Never, ever, ever, try selling the house on your own, figuring you'll save all that money on commission. What a good agent can do is drum up multiple offers, for example, which would more than pay for the commission, and probably for a new bathroom as well.
- How do you find an agent? The easiest way is to cruise the neighbourhood, checking out For Sale signs to see who the local achiever is. If you invite several agents to compete for your business, never choose the one who gives you the highest potential asking price. It's usually a cheap trick. Effective, but still cheap.

The case against real estate

Once again, I affirm my love of real estate. Again, I take issue with all the media chumps who have cast me as a foe of home ownership; that's not the case. But I do believe most people buy the wrong kinds of real estate, finance it badly, hang on to it for too long, believe mistakenly that it will reward them as it did their parents, and are blind to what's coming in the future. Today, about half of all the people who own houses in Canada have no mortgage, and are sitting on hundreds of billions of dollars in equity. That money is not paying them any income, and the only way it is working for them is if the home is increasing in value.

Real estate values and prices are dictated by supply and demand. Real estate, unlike stocks or mutual funds, is illiquid. You can sell a financial asset in a day, or even hours. You can't sell your home until you market it, find a qualified buyer and wait for closing day, hoping the sale will actually go through.

Supply and demand—it's a complicated thing. If too many houses are for sale at the same time, the competition brings prices down. If mortgage rates jump, sales activity falls. If the economy tanks and jobs are lost, buyer enthusiasm dries up. Conversely, if the economy's humming, mortgage rates are reasonable and consumer confidence is high, a bidding war can break out and someone can end up spending far more for a home than the seller asked. This is a constantly changing landscape, in which both buyers and sellers are buffeted by forces they cannot control.

Some people, of course, have done extremely well by investing in real estate, and there will always be winners. But there will also be lots of losers, especially, I believe, in about ten years. This is because the makeup of the population is changing, and because inflation is being wrung out of the system. Why does real estate, especially some specific kinds of it, have a questionable future?

- The nature of families is changing. According to Statistics Canada, the size of the average household is dropping, and will be down to 2.4 people by the year 2016. At the same time, the number of people who will be living alone is set to explode by 70% in the future, rising to almost four million households by 2016.

  The number of two-person households will double, from just over three million in the late nineties to almost six million in 2016. This kind of family will, at 55% of all families, constitute the largest single group. The same trend will take place with single-parent families as their numbers rise by half, with 60% of them headed by women. Finally, a quarter of all Canadians now expect their parents to live with them when they become older.

  These demographic changes mean that the numbers of

potential consumers for traditional multi-bedroom real estate are going to evaporate somewhat, which will have a negative impact on vast tracts of suburban housing designed for the families of another, older, time.

- The population is aging fast. Canada has the highest proportion of Boomers of any nation in the world. In the 1970s, as all those twenty-five-year-olds were getting married and forming families, they ignited a real estate boom. In the eighties, as they moved up and competed for houses and financing, they drove home prices and mortgage rates to historic high levels. In Toronto, it would take twelve years for the price of an average home to rise again to 1989 levels.

Today, nine million Boomers are turning fifty. At that age they have largely finished raising kids, and are entering their peak income-earning years. They are also the healthiest fifty-year-olds in history and will generally live between twenty and thirty years beyond retirement. Most of them, about 70%, will retire with no corporate pension, and rely on a combination of Canada Pension Plan payments (about $8,000 a year if it survives) and their own retirement savings. The average Boomer in 2001 had about $50,000 tucked away in RRSPs, and the vast bulk of personal net worth was tied up in residential real estate.

By 2015, most Boomers will be hitting age sixty-five and will constitute the largest wave of retirees ever to hit Canadian society. Those people who do not gain the windfall of an inheritance will be facing a bleak retirement. Either they will try to continue to work or they will consider unlocking the equity in their greatest asset—their home.

Remember what dictates the price of a home: supply and demand. Now imagine 2015.

- Inflation is dead.

One other significant reason that real estate has performed so well over the last thirty years has been inflation, which raised commodity prices—gold, lumber, houses.

Inflation was the result of a number of factors, such as excessive government spending and deficit financing, which put pressure on the money supply. Inflationary expectations caused a wage-price spiral. So long as the economy was growing rapidly, inflation was just an irritating by-product of good times. But when the economy turned down, as happened in the early nineties, the higher interest rates it had caused were a killer of jobs and a deflator of real estate prices.

In the twenty-first century, governments no longer run deficits but are instead in massive surpluses. The United States in 2000, for the first time in seventy years, was not issuing new bonds but buying them back. Interest rates have been in a downward spiral, with the occasional temporary spike higher, and inflation is down for the count.

The Bank of Canada maintains a target inflation range of between 1% and 3%, and for years the core inflation rate has been at the lower end of that range. From time to time the people who watch over the money supply worry we will slip from inflation to deflation. Actually, some commodities are truly in a deflationary mode: computers, electronic components, cars, even bandwidth. Modern technology, as it turns out, could be the greatest deflator of all.

Without inflation, there is no economic upward pressure on real estate prices, as there was for the Boomers' parents. From here on in, only supply and demand will dictate housing values, and the results could be wildly surprising.

So, the eighties are not coming back. The value of all residential real estate will not steadily rise, making home ownership a universally winning strategy. There will be hot pockets and demand neighbourhoods where people will always pay a premium to live. But there will also be large areas where buyers will not go.

Unconditional advice

The personal finance columnist for *Chatelaine* magazine recently took strong exception to advice I gave on television that buying a house conditional upon getting mortgage financing was a dumb idea. "Bad mortgage advice!" she whined, arguing that this was a dangerous move that could destroy a family's finances. Poor woman.

- To buy a property in a demand area often means going up against competing bidders. Key decisions on the offer price have to be made in minutes, not days or even hours. A successful bidder must be completely prepared, which includes knowing what size of mortgage he or she can, or is willing to, carry.
- To get that knowledge, secure a mortgage pre-approval. It costs nothing. It will tell you precisely how much financing you can afford. And it guarantees your interest rate for a period of sixty or ninety days.
- You can get pre-approved in your bank branch, or on-line with any major lender. This will allow you to completely eliminate any financing condition, and make the offer to purchase clean and strong.

The right real estate strategy

Let me tell you about my real estate, as I have made careful choices. I chose to get rid of a beautiful stone home in a prestigious area of midtown Toronto on a street lined with houses fetching well over a million dollars. I downsized, and at the same time spent a small fortune building a home in the forest, on a river, an hour's drive away.

I spend long hours on Bay Street, running a company I founded that produces television shows and operates a broadcast centre. But commuting is not an option in a city that is forecast to have 35% more cars within the next ten years. Already the average commute in Toronto, one-way, is seventy minutes. Soon that will be ninety, which means suburban dwellers will routinely have to set aside three hours a day for travel. This is one reason suburban real estate sells at such a discount compared with urban properties, and why the gulf will continue to grow.

But while my vocation is in the city these days, my heart is not. Hence my place in the woods. But why tie up a million dollars in a city property that's used four days a week? And why not cash out of the kind of home that relatively few people can afford to buy, and that may be an expensive white elephant in another decade?

So, I sold the kind of home now that may be tough to sell later. I moved my capital into the two kinds of real estate that I believe have a strong future: a very private all-year recreational property within an easy drive of the city core, and a no-care freehold townhouse with a backyard and underground parking, fifteen minutes off Bay Street. In the country I am comfortable and self-sufficient behind a gate I can open via the Internet, with a propane-powered backup electric generator, garden, wells, and a steep driveway that uses landing-pad technology to burn off winter snow. It has a separate guest-house apartment for visitors and is five minutes from the grocery store and seventeen from a hospital. I believe in a decade it would sell overnight. But I don't think I'll list it.

In the city, my condo townhouse is twenty feet wide and three storeys tall. It's four minutes from the subway and just off a major route leading downtown to the bank towers and uptown to the highways. Gardeners for the complex take care of the grass and flowers. In the winter the snow's removed, and underneath is heated indoor parking. Garbage disappears from the back door twice a week, and yet I have my own fenced and landscaped backyard, which the dog loves and protects. The condo fees are cheap, the taxes a third of what I was paying at my old stone home, and I bought it for less than half what I sold the detached home for, just a few streets away. I believe in a decade this too would sell overnight. It has a huge universe of potential buyers who can afford it, and who want the convenience and the location.

There is smart real estate, there is excessive real estate, and there is real estate that has no future. There's a reason why tiny, sixty-year-old, 800-square-foot bungalows along forested streets in midtown Toronto sell for $350,000 to $400,000 while brand new housing in the suburbs, three times the size, can be yours for less. The bungalows represent what people want: location, convenience and quality of life. Walk to public transit and the bank. Access to established schools. Big old trees. This housing sells in hours, despite the condition of the homes, because buyers know you can always renovate but never re-create.

Today, the right real estate strategy starts with a recognition of where true value lies when it comes to housing in the future. There are some kinds of homes that will actually decline in value as the universe of potential buyers shrinks. A prime example is a multi-bedroom monster house with a three-car garage, Scarlett O'Hara staircase, and pool in the backyard, in a distant suburb accessible from downtown only by spending gruelling hours on an eight-lane "expressway."

As the average family shrinks in size and the population ages; as more people determine clearly that they want to be urban dwellers or nature lovers; as cities find it increasingly impossible to modernize and add to their transit infrastructures, real estate tastes will keep on changing.

So while the housing market today is relatively robust, thanks to a decent economy and cheap mortgage rates, the time is ideal to cash out of housing that has a cloudy future. Meanwhile, the time is always right to be buying what others will want, and value, in the future. That could be an inner-city bungalow, a well-located, carefree townhome or semi, a property in an adult community on a golf course or lake, a condominium (two bedrooms instead of four), a self-sufficient and secure country home, or an age-proofed home with wide hallways, lots of light, few stairs, and a voice-activated home management software installation.

In terms of investment real estate, do not make the mistake of buying a single residential unit to rent out. Today, virtually any single home or condo unit will not fetch enough money to pay much more than the mortgage, so you are basically just turning over dollars. That cash is better put into a hard-working equity mutual fund. About the only income-producing real estate I would consider now and into the future would be a multiple-unit apartment building. It can generally be bought with a small down payment, and can give you positive cash flow from day one, plus the ability to remortgage it in the future, taking out tax-free cash.

Think ahead. Choose wisely. The wrong property could be your own personal wealth trap.

Tax-free housing

> The most compelling argument for owning a principal residence is its tax-free status when you sell it. No capital gains tax bill will materialize, so if you are lucky enough to sell for more than you paid, owning residential real estate can make sense. Obviously, picking the right property is essential. Think resale the day you make the offer.
> - To get tax-free status, a house has to be declared your principal residence, which means you must prove it's the place providing you and your family's main accommodation.
> - This does not mean you can't own two houses that you occupy on a regular basis. It simply means you can't sell them both in the same year and claim tax-free status on both.
> - It is also possible to have tax-free status on a property you or your spouse have owned since before 1982. Back then, each spouse was allowed to have a principal (tax-free) residence, provided each house was, in fact, regularly lived in—which means a summer cottage would qualify. You need to establish what the value of that piece of property was at the end of 1981.

Living in volatile times

I'm old enough to remember October 19, 1987. It was one hairy day. There was no organized Internet then, or computer tracking of the stock markets, so I watched the meltdown of the New York Stock Exchange on a tape-spewing Dow Jones newswire machine in my editor's office at a major Toronto daily newspaper.

By the end of the day the market had lost 508.32 points, or 22.6% of its entire value. More than 600 million shares, a record, had changed hands, and investors had taken a $750-million haircut. I thought I'd seen it all. In fact, a lot of people believed that day would turn into a rerun of 1929, after such stunning volatility on the market.

Well, today we know better. Volatility stalks the land as never before. Constant, daily market churning now makes the quick lurch lower at the end of the eighties look like a crude event indeed. These days we routinely see a billion shares change hands in a single trading day in New York. In less than a year, the technology-laden NASDAQ fell from over 5,000 to less than 2,000. In fifty weeks, giant Nortel Networks lost 90% of its value. The Dow can shed or gain 500 points on a Thursday and it barely makes the front page.

The times have never been more volatile than they are now, and it is no phenomenon. It's normal, it's routine—and it's the future.

Why has it happened? Volatility is the result of human progress and the ongoing technological revolution. As Ray Perryman, of the Houston-based Perryman Group, wrote:

> It is a long-known and widely accepted dictum among economists and investors that greater knowledge makes markets more efficient. Indeed, the immediate and costless availability of all pertinent information is a

> requirement for efficient markets. The fallacy in the minds of many is to equate "efficiency" with "stability." They are not the same thing. As markets become more sophisticated and have greater access to data, they will set prices more frequently.

Exactly. Information is to blame. It is at the root of all volatility, as people react to new knowledge. As Perryman points out, when the telephone and telegraph brought more information and international currency supply and demand, exchange rates went volatile. As satellites flashed back earth images showing crop yields, commodity prices started to fluctuate by the minute.

Today we have the ultimate information pipeline: the Internet. Information about companies, their stock and the markets it trades on has never been so great, flowed so quickly or ended up in the hands of so many end-users. As the investment ground shifts second to second, so prices are reset and markets respond. They have never been as efficient as they are now at reflecting known change, and that translates into the kind of volatility that can cream an unsuspecting investor.

As Wall Street Strategies CEO Charles Payne put it:

> It boils down to the confluence of two technology-driven trends. The World Wide Web and a plethora of financial Web sites have made it possible for near-instantaneous dissemination of market-moving information. Similarly, investors now have the ability to react immediately to news by way of on-line trading accounts, electronic communications systems and other technological innovations. As a result, wild price gyrations, which in the past took weeks or months to play out, are now compressed into minutes or days.

And who is reacting to that? Who drives the market? There are three groups: institutions, individual investors and daytraders. Of course daytraders would not exist without the technology that allows information to be pumped into their terminals every nanosecond. They buy and sell stocks over the course of hours, or sometimes even minutes, taking advantage of the momentum and price fluctuations caused by volatility. Most of them try to end their days in cash, rather than risk hanging on to a stock overnight.

As daytrader Ken Wolff wrote in an article for TheStreet.com:

> We daytraders create our own type of momentum. I always set top priority on cheaper stocks, unless I'm seeing big moves from the more expensive stocks. I watch how stocks are reacting to news in the short term and how strong the bounces are at the tops and bottoms of intraday oscillations. We daytraders run in cycles; we come and go with the tide. At times I will go into buying frenzies. When this happens I hold a bit longer, but other times I sell quickly at the first sign of weakness and have to fight for every quarter-point.

Even more powerful market-makers are the millions of average investors who today play the market through on-line brokerage accounts, where you can buy or sell with a single click of the mouse, and often for a cheap, discounted trading fee. These millions of people executing billions of trades also have full access to the latest breaking news that the pros on Bay Street and Wall Street read. The complete and total democratization of the markets has taken place, bringing with it incredible opportunity, stunning danger and more volatility than could even have been imagined a decade ago. Ten years ago, investors held NASDAQ stocks for an average of two years; today that's down to five months.

These days, investors will buy and sell on rumour, speculation, gossip or some ill-informed comments posted on an Internet chat board. It all contributes to a thinly controlled conflagration known as the market—where your stock portfolio, mutual fund or RRSP happens to live.

How can you find investment peace in volatile times? You have two choices:

- Think long-term. Ignoring volatility is the course of least resistance. Keep your eye on the big picture, on macroeconomics and long-term trends. If you believe in the Long Wave, then you know that over the next ten or fifteen years we will see rising markets thanks to technology, demographics, falling inflation, interest rates and taxes, global free trade and economic expansion. So what if the NASDAQ loses half its value in six months, since it will be vastly higher by 2010? All you need to do is hang on.

    This means you should be diversified, investing in equity mutual funds instead of individual stocks. It also means asset allocation is important to minimize risk. If preserving your capital is the most important goal, then put 10% in stocks, 60% in bonds and 20% in cash. But if you are a believer in the future, and an aggressive investor, then head 80% into equities and 10% each in bonds and cash. The first step is setting a realistic goal that is truly reflective of your own tolerance for risk and desire for wealth. Over time, as history shows us, money grows nowhere so fast as in equities.

    If you fear volatility, don't invest money you'll need for something else in the short term. Don't invest more than you're comfortable investing. Don't invest borrowed money, especially on a margin account. Don't panic and sell at the first sign of weakness. Don't rip open the financial section every morning and track the value of your stocks and mutual funds.

    The best strategy is to get a financial adviser who will recommend a diversified portfolio that over the course of the next decade or so will achieve your financial goals. Then forget about it.

Or, of course, you could…

- Think short-term. Volatility can be as empowering as it is endangering. Without volatility there would not be market momentum nor the phenomenon of daytrading. When markets correct, it can create giant opportunities. While buying a stock that is falling in a rising market is bad news, in a crashing market all stocks tend to be demolished, offering an unparalleled opportunity to buy at a discount, or to average down the costs of existing holdings.

  Look back at the last three massive buying opportunities: the Asian flu of the summer of 1998, the Y2K crisis of late 1999, and the tech wreck of 2000–2001. All gave investors the opportunity of picking up great companies and well-run, well-invested mutual funds at a fraction of the price commanded just months before, or months after. So it is ironic that millions of people sat on billions of dollars in cash in low-yielding accounts during all three events, driven to inaction and nervous paralysis by the wrong advice.

  Short-term investors, in contrast, can take volatility and make it work for them. Trailing stop losses can protect the downside in active markets. Put options can achieve the same goal.

  And then there is the beauty of short-selling. If you are sure the market, or an individual stock, will be heading lower, you can make money by selling it short. This means borrowing the stock from a broker, selling it first and then buying it back later, at a lower price. Sell Nortel at $124, buy it back at $12, and make $112 a share. That's the strategy, and it would have worked exactly like that between the fall of 2000 and the summer of 2001. This is clearly not for everyone, but it's tangible proof that as much, or more, money can be made in a market that's in free fall as in one exploding higher.

Volatility is here to stay. If you panic and sell at the wrong moment, it will destroy your wealth. If you succumb to euphoria and buy at the wrong time, you are in extreme danger. If you ignore volatility, diversify and adopt the long view, you will prosper. If you ride the beast, you will never forget it.

Can you live without art?

I doubt I'll forget the moment Ken Thomson paid $2.2 million for a Lawren Harris painting. It was the most anyone, anywhere, had ever paid for a Canadian work of art, and it was about double what the auctioneer had estimated the thing was worth that night in early 2001. But it was a tangible demonstration that art is a commodity just like real estate and gold, one that investors can get seriously bothered over. Some tips:
- If you have the stomach for it, buy your art at auction. That way, you know you're paying the market price—plus the buyer's premium, which is the 15% or so the auction house adds on.
- Don't be there. I've found the best way to go after a painting is to bid by telephone. You can focus just on the money you're willing to pay, and not on the competition building within the auction room.
- Buy Canadian. The experts believe that our art is vastly undervalued compared with American works, especially sculpture. Prices have shot dramatically higher in recent years, as Mr. Thomson will attest. A William Kurelek that changed hands for less than $40,000 a few years ago sold in 2001 for $299,000.

Why you should have RRSPs

RRSPs are not products, but vehicles allowing you to push current tax bills off into the distant future while holding assets you could own anyway and enjoying far more rapid growth. If more Canadians understood this, they would go RRSP nuts.

Most people today don't have an RRSP, and those who do

have a tiny amount of money in there—less than $50,000. Considering the average age of an RRSP owner is almost forty-five, we are clearly not using the muscle of this thing to build wealth.

There are two reasons you must have RRSPs:

- Every dollar you contribute comes off your taxable income. This is a huge gift from the government to encourage you to save and invest. It's such a good deal that it's socially irresponsible. The more money you make, the bigger your writeoff. So a taxpayer earning $85,000 is able to contribute $13,500 a year and pay almost $7,000 less in tax, while someone earning $25,000 can contribute only $4,500 and save a mere $1,500 in tax.

   Is that fair? Of course not. It's a subsidy to the well off, which is why big changes to RRSPs are inevitable. It's also why you can't afford to let this opportunity go by.
- Every dollar inside your RRSP will not be taxed on the money it earns. That means a GIC paying you 6% actually gives you 6%, instead of the after-tax 3% you would earn outside the plan. So, money in here grows twice as fast and can multiply like bunnies in April.

The idea behind the RRSP is simple: put money away now with the ability to write it off your taxable income; shelter it from tax, so it will grow quickly over several decades; then take the money out to live on when you are retired. At that point you must pay income tax on the withdrawals, but probably at a lower tax rate, for two reasons: first, most people retire on less income than they earned while working, so they pay tax at a lower rate; second, income taxes across North America are falling rapidly, so the odds are high that RRSP money socked away today will be less taxed when it comes out in, say, 2020.

The limit on your annual RRSP contribution is 18% of what you earned the year before, to a max of $13,500 (which should be increasing soon). To write it off your taxable income for a particular year, the contribution has to be made before the first sixty days of the next year have expired. But smart people contribute at the beginning of every year for that taxation year, so the money compounds tax-free for a longer period of time.

Here are two strategies for making an RRSP contribution even when you don't have any extra cash:

- Borrow the money the right way. You can get an RRSP loan at any financial institution for the prime rate, which is low and will be going lower still over the next five years. Invest it inside the RRSP in growth mutual funds.

    When you get your tax refund, use it to pay down the bank loan (many lenders will not even charge you loan interest until you get that refund). Now you have used the government's money to pay off up to half the loan for an investment that you own entirely—not a bad deal. Yes, another subsidy.
- Make a contribution in kind. This is my favourite strategy, because it is so simple, effective and incredible.

    The rules allow you to use assets instead of money to make an RRSP contribution. In other words, you can take things you already own—like mutual funds, bonds, stocks or GICs—and just transfer them into your RRSP. To do so, you will need to have a self-directed plan (which your financial adviser or bank can set up in a snap).

    Now here's the incredible part: for selling yourself assets that you already own, the government will credit you with a tax refund that equals as much as half the value of the assets themselves. So, take a bond worth $10,000 and transfer it into your plan, and you will receive a refund worth up to $5,000. Now you have the equivalent of $15,000, of which $10,000 is sheltered from taxes that you previously had to pay on the interest it earned. Another subsidy.

So, it certainly makes sense every year to transfer as many assets as you can into your RRSP (up to your contribution limit), so you can simply put an end to paying taxes every year on your investments!

There are many more strategies for making the most of your registered retirement plan, like having your RRSP actually hold the mortgage on your home, so you make mortgage payments to yourself. You can find complete details in one of my annual RRSP guides. But the important thing to realize is that this government program blatantly favours people with incomes, investments and wealth. For many lower-income people RRSPs are useless, because they can actually live better in retirement off government handouts. But for every middle-class Canadian, an RRSP is the ticket to serious tax reduction and a subsidized investment strategy.

While it is still there to grab, grab hard.

Money for nothing

All RRSPs are not created equal. The best kind is a self-directed RRSP and the worst is the kind most people have—a GIC-type savings plan run for you by your financial institution. If you have one of these:

- Hook up with a financial adviser and have him or her open a self-directed plan, and then handle the transfer of funds from your bank plan into the new one. The adviser will do this for you without cost, and often will even pay any transfer fee the bank charges, just to get your business.
- Or, you can open a self-directed plan yourself and have the money transferred over. The advantage of this kind of RRSP is that you can put in it just about any asset you own—stocks, bonds, mutual funds or GICs included.
- Every year, a good strategy is to take assets you already own outside the RRSP and transfer them into the self-directed plan, up to the limit of your contribution room. For making this "contribution in kind," the feds will send you a tax refund. Yes, money for nothing.

Why RRSPs can be a terrible idea

There is one horrible, troubling aspect to RRSPs: when the money comes out, it is taxed.

Now, if you retire on a pittance and stay in a low tax bracket, this is merely irritating. However, if you retire on an income of $60,000 or more, it amounts to a financial mugging. You will be handing over half of your entire retirement nest egg in tax, wiping away the advantage you received years earlier when you made tax-deductible contributions.

Compare this to the tax you'd pay in retirement on assets that were giving you income in the form of capital gains outside your RRSP. As explained elsewhere in this volume, the capital gains inclusion rate has been reduced to 50%, which means you need pay tax only on half of the profit you make from things like stocks and mutual funds. That means, even for the taxpayer in the highest tax bracket (roughly 50%), the maximum capital gains tax rate will be half of 50%, or just 25%.

So, for higher-income retirees, the choice is simple: give up half of your RRSPs in tax, or keep 75% of the capital gains outside your RRSP. If you need help making that decision, check your pulse.

Since the big drop in capital gains tax in the pre-election budget of 2000, many people who know they will have a healthy retirement income should get money out of their plans. The trouble is, of course, that withdrawals are taxable. Fortunately, there is a strategy to get around that problem. It's called an RRSP meltdown—a way of taking money out of your plan and getting it invested outside without triggering additional tax. Here's the plan:

- Borrow money to invest in assets (like equity mutual funds) that will yield you a long-term capital gain. Let's make it a $100,000 loan, at an interest rate of 8%, which means $8,000 a year in interest-only payments.
- Finance those interest payments by withdrawing money from your RRSP (or your RRIF).
- The RRSP withdrawals are still fully taxable, but the interest payments on the investment loan are fully tax-deductible. That means you have to declare $8,000 in taxable income, but you also have the right to deduct $8,000 in interest expense from your taxable income.
- The bottom line: you pay no additional tax, even though you have used RRSP money to finance a $100,000 investment portfolio outside your RRSP. The idea is that over time you will drain cash out of your registered plan and replace it with money that will yield you capital gains at one-half the tax rate you'd have faced otherwise.

How do you know if an RRSP meltdown strategy is right for you? The simplest way is to get some help from a financial adviser, who will make that determination for you, looking at likely retirement income from investments, pensions and government programs, and then deciding if you already have too much money sitting in an RRSP. Certainly, if it looks like your retirement income will be high, the decision is a simple one: start melting.

And what should an overall RRSP strategy be, given the conflicts inherent in the advice on the last few pages? Here it is:

(1) When you start earning income, max out your RRSP contributions. This will defer tax for decades to come, increase your take-home pay (if you make monthly contributions and get payroll taxes reduced as a result) and start your lifetime investment program.

(2) Make sure you always put your RRSP capital into growth assets, like equity or index mutual funds, not into low-yielding things like savings bonds or guaranteed investment certificates.

(3) In your forties, you should have an idea of what your retirement income might be, just as you are hitting your peak income-earning years (typically between the ages of forty-five and fifty-four). This is the time to start reconsidering the wisdom of making any more RRSP contributions, and to be building up capital gains–yielding investments outside your registered plan.

(4) Ten years prior to retirement, assuming your income will keep you in the top tax bracket, work with your adviser to melt down RRSP assets in a way that does not trigger additional tax, as outlined above.

Over the long haul I think it's a safe bet that the rate of tax on RRSPs will actually go up (as the inherent unfairness of the system is corrected), while tax on capital gains income will continue to fall (to stimulate the economy as Boomers age). Recognize that now and position yourself to take maximum benefit.

My advice in a nutshell: Exploit RRSPs. Defer tax and build wealth. Then melt and escape.

What to shelter

> When do RRSPs make real investment sense? When you are risk-averse and insist on putting a substantial amount of your wealth into interest-bearing investments.
> - The tax burden on interest, salary and pension income in this country is extreme, despite recent moves by the federal and provincial governments to slash tax rates. In general, you will pay twice the rate of tax on a dollar earned as interest compared with the same dollar earned as a capital gain.
> - So, put things like bonds and GICs inside an RRSP to defer tax, and allow them to compound tax-free. Remember, with investments like strip bonds or Canada Savings Bonds, you are required to pay an annual tax bill even though the interest has yet to be paid to you.

- Hold mutual funds and stocks outside your plan, since the maximum tax payable will be 25%. In retirement, your tax bill on these investments will be half of that on the money you are forced to withdraw from a RRIF.

Buy the Boom

It must be easy to hate the Baby Boomers. The influence of this group has been overwhelming for the past fifty years—overrunning the schools, causing a huge infrastructure bill for governments, planting the seeds of the national debt, driving up interest rates and real estate values, then fuelling the mutual fund and stock market explosion. Music, culture and even clothing and cars have been defined by the millions born between 1946 and 1967, and the process continues today. The redesigned Volkswagen Beetle, the reborn Austin Mini and Ford Thunderbird, the retro packaging of the Chrysler PT Cruiser and the renaissance of the classic Harley-Davidson motorcycle all owe their market presence to the Boomers' tastes and backgrounds. Anticipating what this generation wants, and catering to it, is big business today, just as it's been for the last four decades.

If you had been able to anticipate the Boomers' coming influence on inflation, mortgage rates and housing prices in the early eighties, you could have made a killing. Similarly, in the early nineties, as the leading edge of the generation passed into its forties, if you'd realized what the Boomers would do to funds and equities, creating a decade-long raging bull market, you might have scored.

Today, you have the same opportunity to harness demographics for profit, as the Boomers move into their fifties and beyond. Over the next five years, aging Boomers will constitute the bulk of population growth by age group in Canada and the United States. In the States, the 55-to-64 age group will be the fastest-growing, with five million people joining it. Next will be those between 45 and 54, up about three and a half million. This compares with an actual decline in the number of people aged 25 to 44. The consequences of this decline are fairly obvious: fewer people in their prime home-buying years, leading to a softer real estate market and, likely, declining mortgage rates. That supports my beliefs about the future of residential housing.

What's next for the Boomers? What will be the Next Big Thing, and how do we turn it into opportunity?

Typically, people aged 45 to 60 have higher incomes than any other age group. In fact the peak earning and spending years are between 45 and 54, when the average income is almost 50% higher than the national norm. This group also tends to have far fewer children to care for, and therefore more disposable income as they actively prepare for a retirement that is clearly on the horizon, and will last a long time.

And then there is the issue of inheritances. Today, millions of Boomers across North America have parents in their seventies and eighties, and they will be receiving an estimated $3 trillion over the next decade from family estates—the largest intergenerational transfer of wealth in human history. Another reality of this age group is that eight out of ten people between the ages of 50 and 60 own their own homes, and a majority of them have no mortgage.

So, the snapshot is becoming clearer: Over the next decade the largest single age group in the Canadian and American populations will have more wealth and income, and less debt, than at any other time in their lives. Demand for both mortgages and real estate will decline. This should have a calming effect on inflation, and help lead to lower interest rates for years to come.

Facing the highest life expectancy in history, with thirty to forty more years ahead of them—most of them not working—the Boomers have a huge need for wealth accumulation and, in an environment of low rates, little alternative but to be active investors, especially since the majority will retire without corporate pensions.

This will all take place in an economic environment we can already see strongly emerging—a time of little inflation, when the cost of money is falling and rapid technological advances are making every industry more productive. Globalization and free trade will lead to stronger economies and rapid export growth. Personal tax rates should be falling steadily as Western governments record strong budget surpluses and start repaying accumulated public debts. In short, the Boomers will score again.

As William Sterling, co-author of the hit book *Boomernomics* (and co-manager of the mutual fund of the same name), has written:

> If we are correct to expect that inflation will remain low based on sensible central banking, intense global competition and ongoing technological progress, then there is no reason to believe that interest rates or stock valuations such as P/E ratios will revert to the mean any time soon. If anything, we still believe that interest rates could fall to surprisingly low levels during this decade, which implies the continuation of fairly rich valuation levels in equity markets.

All this would strongly suggest that the tech wreck of late 2000 and 2001 was a cyclical bear market following an unsustainable bubble, and not some secular bear market with a long lifespan and bitter effects. That means the down market—any down market that takes place over the next few years, for that matter—is nothing more than a buying opportunity. The economic and demographic fundamentals are simply too strong for any sustained downturn. There will be too much money in the hands of too many motivated people, who will constitute the largest and healthiest bunch of 50- and 60-year-olds in history, not to have robust financial markets.

What does that mean? Quite possibly the Dow Jones and the TSE at 20,000, or much more, by the end of 2005, along with a spectacular rebound for the technology-laden NASDAQ. It means great opportunity for investors in the financial services sector, as well as science and technology and health sciences, including biotechnology. And as the Boomers reach their more conservative years, it will be time for smart investors to learn a whole lot more about bonds.

A dumb idea

> Author David Chilton made a personal fortune from sales of his book *The Wealthy Barber*. David offers a great example of how to profit from demographics, since his simplistic guide to the basics of financial planning was published just as the Boomers had figured out that there was more to security than buying a house. Millions of people bought the book and benefited from doing so.
>
> One of David Chilton's key *Wealthy Barber* strategies was dollar-cost averaging, which means investing a set amount on a regular basis to cope with market volatility. In a month when markets are down, your $500 buys more mutual fund units than when things are on a tear. But here's why I think it's a dumb idea:
> - Dollar-cost averaging is really a crude attempt at timing the markets. Over an extended period of time, and when (as today) the economic fundamentals are positive, markets will generally go up in value. Therefore, serious long-term investors should not hold back on putting in whatever they've earmarked for equities.
> - The most important thing you can do is to spend as long as possible in a diversified equity investment. So, instead of allocating a little money each month from your income stream, borrow a whack of it, make tax-deductible, interest-only monthly payments with the money you would otherwise use for dollar-cost averaging, and marvel at how much better off you will be in five years.

The Next Big Thing

Bonds. The Canadian corporate and government bond market is thirty times bigger than the stock market and a dozen times bigger than the entire economy. Every year, about $12 trillion in debt changes hands, and every major brokerage company has huge bond trading departments, which are largely hidden from the sight, and the awareness, of individual Canadian investors.

This will change. In fact it has already started, with the advent of a Web site where you can buy and sell bonds, as well as new index units based on Government of Canada securities. More on those opportunities in a minute, but first a few words about these securities, which will, as the Boomers age and their need to retain wealth becomes paramount, get huge.

Corporations and governments issue bonds to raise long-term money. With corporations, this is often preferable to issuing more shares, since selling stock dilutes the holdings of all existing shareholders and broadens the ownership of the company. A bond is simply an obligation (*obligation*, in fact, is the French word for "bond") to repay money borrowed on a certain day in the future (the maturity date) and to pay interest (the coupon rate) on that money in the meantime.

These are vastly different animals from Canada Savings Bonds because they can give you a regular income stream, as well as a capital gain, since the value of a bond is constantly fluctuating, influenced by many things, but mostly by changes in interest rates. In general, government bonds are more secure than corporate bonds and therefore pay slightly less interest. Since it is now in a surplus position and doesn't need more money than it raises from taxes, the federal government no longer issues bonds. However, there are lots of "Canada bonds" already in existence, changing hands daily, and these will be around for at least two decades to come. And provinces continue to issue their own bonds, along with provincial utilities and Crown corporations. You can also buy corporate bonds and the debt of other countries in bond form.

Bonds can be incredibly secure if you want them to be. In other words, if you buy a bond for $100,000 and hold it to maturity, you know you'll get $100,000 on a certain day in the future. Meanwhile, you also know it will pay you interest every six months. So, if you were to purchase six bonds with staggered maturity dates, you could construct a "bond ladder" and receive monthly income for pretty well your entire retirement, with lump sums flowing in at known times.

Therefore, a bond portfolio can give you security, income and predictability. But bonds can also give you more—capital gains, just like stocks or mutual funds that rise in value. If you buy a $10,000 bond for $10,000, then you have bought it "at par." The advantage will be the income stream it gives you until the day of maturity. If the coupon rate is 8%, then you get $800 a year in interest. However, most investors don't hold bonds for that long, nor are they generally bought on the day of issue, so let's call them used bonds. With used bonds, the price will vary according to prevailing interest rates and the length of time to maturity. If the bond was issued with a coupon rate of 6%, for example, and current interest rates are 5.5%, then the bond is worth more. Conversely, if rates have risen since the bond was issued, you can buy it at a discount to its face value. The price you pay ends up affecting the actual yield to maturity (YTM) of the bond. The less you pay for a bond, the higher its YTM.

Bond prices move in the opposite direction to interest rates. When rates rise, bonds cheapen because they have a fixed coupon rate. But when rates fall, as has been the case and will likely continue, bonds grow more valuable. Bond prices rise and fall daily on the expectation of what rates might do.

Long bonds are more volatile than short ones. You can buy a bond that matures in just months or in decades, and as the bond gets near its maturity date, swings in value are less extreme since you know exactly what it will pay you in the near term. Bonds can also come with special features, such as a call provision for having it mature sooner, or an extendible maturity, and these features will affect the price you pay.

Why will bonds be much bigger news going forward? Simply because government and corporate bonds offer many of the advantages of stocks and mutual funds (income, capital gains, tradability and liquidity) without the disadvantages (market crashes, capital losses and stress). Bonds are fundamentally more secure than equities, and in the case of government bonds there is absolutely no risk. If a Canada bond were to fail to pay you on maturity, then there would be no Canada. Period.

How do you enter this world of fixed-income trading? The easiest way is to open an account with one of the bank-owned investment dealers like RBC Capital Markets, ScotiaMcLeod or Nesbitt Burns. They all have monstrously big bond trading departments and access to every security on the market. Of course you can also try to do it yourself. E-bond (www.ebond.ca) is currently the leading on-line discount dealer that allows direct buying and selling. You can check out its retail bond prices there or get the market bid/ask prices at a Web site like Can PX (www.canpx.ca).

There are also mutual funds that buy bonds, and you can purchase these easily through any financial adviser, bank or on-line discount broker. The advantage is that bond funds can buy a lot more than you could and generally get a better deal. The downside is that the funds aren't set up to hold bonds to maturity, so the fund manager trades actively in the hope of getting capital gains. So, there's volatility—as well as management fees—to consider.

There are also index units now available. Barclays Global launched the first two exchange-traded funds (ETFs) in 2000, which mirror government bond returns. The iG5 and iG10 mimic five-year and ten-year bonds and have low management expense ratios of just 0.25%.

Despite these bond-type products, however, aging Boomers with a fairly serious portfolio will want to be direct bond junkies. You can establish a portfolio that gives you regular, predictable income, with securities that turn into cash exactly when you expect them to, and yet still earn low-taxed capital gains if you buy the right bonds in an environment of dropping interest rates. If you buy a quality bond and hold it to maturity, there is no risk, no matter what interest rates might do. And if you put bonds inside an RRSP or a RRIF, then all of the growth is tax-free.

The Next Big Thing, available now.

Bulls, bears and experience

Stock and bond markets are never still. The value of assets traded there is constantly changing, according to supply and demand, fear and greed, perception and reality, rumour and news. Recent market swings have been huge, and it looks like volatility is here to stay. If you follow the markets, here are some common terms to understand:
- A *bull* market is one on the rise over an extended period of time, typically two years or more. A shorter session in which stocks rise is called a *rally*.
- A *bear* market is one in a protracted state of decline—typically lasting a little less than a year, but it can be a lot longer. (It took the Dow about eight years to retake its 1972 high, while the Nikkei in Japan in 2001 was seventeen years off its high.)
- A market *decline* happens when an index falls about 5%. These days, this can happen in an afternoon.
- A *correction* is generally regarded as a 10% pullback, and it is nothing much to worry about since markets tend to get ahead of themselves on a regular basis. A correction is usually a healthy event, and a buying opportunity. A severe correction, of 15%, has happened sixteen times in the last fifty years.
- A *crash* is when panic selling hits and the market suffers a swift 20% loss in just a few days. This has happened only twice in the history of the Dow, in 1929 and 1987. In 1929 it helped lead to a ten-year depression, while in 1987 the market regained all lost ground in about eighteen months—thanks to experience.

Inflation and deflation

In 1935, my father was a schoolteacher in Ontario with an annual salary of $700. In the summer he worked as a highway-builder for $1 a day. A loaf of bread cost a nickel and every month the price of things went down.

As a consequence, he and my mother waited to get married and start a family, since there was no point in buying anything of value because it would be cheaper next year. Two years earlier, in 1933, the American president, F.D. Roosevelt, had outlawed the private ownership of gold by American citizens and devalued the dollar in an attempt to print more money and deal with the greatest economic devil unleashed on humanity: deflation.

In 1980, my parents were retired and invested in hundreds of ounces of silver and in real estate. That silver leapt in value from a few dollars an ounce to $50, pacing a staggering increase in the price of gold. Meanwhile, the value of residential real estate in southern Ontario was soaring, and they got into the habit of buying a home, living in it for two or three years, then selling it for a substantial capital gain. That way they could live for free and still build wealth, thanks to inflation.

Over the course of my father's eighty-five years, inflation was good and deflation was bad. Inflation increased his wealth and ballooned the value of his assets. Deflation was synonymous with poverty, job loss, business failure and misery.

Both inflation and deflation are self-reinforcing economic conditions. When the economy is growing, prices rise along with demand. Workers ask for salary and wage increases to maintain their purchasing power, and that leads to higher business costs, which get reflected in higher prices. Inflation leads to higher valuations for assets like real estate and almost all other commodities, inflating personal wealth. As people come to assume that prices and asset values will continue to rise, inflation becomes an ingrained feature of the landscape. Governments are forced into deficit financing and debt swells out of control, leading to bond issues that put pressure on the money supply, leading to higher interest rates, depressing corporate profits and the stock market.

Deflation too is a self-propelling force. As the price of commodities falls—houses, cars, capital equipment, food, computers—there is a disincentive to spend money buying them; it makes more sense to wait and acquire the assets at a future date for less cash. Decreased demand for commodities and manufactured goods quickly leads to a collapse in business cash flow and profits, an inventory buildup, then layoffs, plant closures and commercial failures. Unemployment swells the workforce, swamping the few jobs available with a massive supply of workers, driving wages and salaries down dramatically, as people are happy to work at anything, for anything. Deflation can collapse an economy, as it did in the 1930s.

So, for the last hundred years or so, life was pretty good when times were inflationary (1920s, 1950s, 1960s and 1980s), not so good when they were disinflationary (1970s and early 1990s) and terrible when they were deflationary (1930s). The unexplained exception seems to be the period from the late 1990s into the 2000s, when inflation was absent, the economy was growing rapidly, and both technology and the stock markets were achieving unimaginable advances. This raises the obvious question of whether or not we have broken the inflation-deflation cycle that gripped the lives of my parents, and are entering into an age when the old economic truths no longer apply.

The answer is probably yes.

Joseph Schumpeter was a Harvard University economist about the time my father was teaching twenty-three students in a one-room school in Oxford County. In 1939, the year my parents decided to get married, and as the world prepared to enter into a war that would re-inflate the economy,

Schumpeter wrote a book called *Business Cycles*. In it he identified three basic rhythms of modern economies: a short inventory cycle of three years, an investment cycle of ten years, and a long wave cycle about two generations in length. He described the Great Depression as the natural result of these rhythms, despite government policies that attempted to change them (FDR's New Deal and the Federal Reserve's move to inflate the money supply).

Schumpeter also came to the conclusion that the modern industrialized world goes through natural periods of inflation and deflation, with deflation being most prominent during those times of revolutionary technological change, such as the railroad/telegraph boom of the 1870s or the automobile/radio boom of the mid-1920s and 1930s. But according to his model, there should have been deflation in the 1980s, when in fact there was inflation. Why the difference?

It's because today, governments attempt to micromanage the economy, constantly influencing interest rates, the money supply, business and consumer demand, to moderate inflation. In fact, central banks in just about every major country in the world, except one, exist to fight inflation, and they have basically succeeded. Only in Japan has deflation emerged as the villain. The Japanese economy has been sinking for a decade following a bout of hyperinflation based on a real estate bubble and fuelled by a corrupt banking system that created unsustainable paper wealth. The cost of money was reduced to zero by an inept Bank of Japan, without stimulating demand or economic growth.

Some people worry that Japanese deflation is a precursor to the same disease in Europe and North America. They believe that personal debt levels and a negative savings rate in the United States have left tens of millions of people vulnerable to instant bankruptcy in any deflationary economic downturn that brings widespread job losses and the inability to make bloated credit card and mortgage payments.

But this is unlikely to happen. Central banks have, in fact, been able to defeat inflation but at the same time maintain economic growth. As the 1990s turned into the new century, and despite rising energy costs, the core inflation rate in Canada and the U.S. remained extremely low. This was, as Schumpeter had reasoned, due to rapid technological innovation. The prices of new labour-saving devices, such as computers, hand-held electronic products, servers and even cars, were pushed lower almost monthly, making businesses more productive. As productivity increased, so did efficiency.

The inflationary stock market bubble that the technology revolution created in 1998 and 1999 was intentionally burst by the same inflation-fighting central bankers, led by Fed chair Alan Greenspan, who raised interest rates deliberately, then backed off to guide the economy into a soft landing, setting the scene for years of growth. Governments chimed in, right on cue, with massive tax cuts in 2001—$100 billion in the U.S. and $40 billion in Canada—giving consumers more money to spend on capital goods while the government presided over record surpluses and debt repayment strategies.

Today, it *is* different. There is reason to believe that the extremes of deflation and inflation which bedevilled the generation now passing will not be visited upon their offspring. If so, this will be a gift of unbridled proportions and staggering consequences.

Why you should get married

> Are you splitting income with your spouse? If the two of you are in different tax brackets, then you should be. Your total family tax bill can be cut by using one of these strategies:
> - Open a spousal RRSP. You're allowed to put all of your own annual RRSP contribution into the name of your spouse, and after three years he/she owns it. You get to deduct the money from your (higher) income and he/she gets to withdraw it at a lower tax rate.
> - If you make the most money in your household, then you should pay the family expenses. Your spouse, who makes less and is in a lower

tax bracket, should be the investor in the family. Capital gains in his/her hands will be taxed more lightly than in yours.
- In retirement, apply to split CPP benefits with your spouse instead of having them melt away in the hands of the person making the most.
- Give your sweetie money to open a business. None of the profits will be taxable for you. Your spouse gets to deduct all business expenses, including a portion of your mortgage and household costs, if it's based at home.

The myth of risk

No doubt about it, I've had an interesting life. Journalist, entrepreneur, politician, then author, broadcaster, speaker, columnist and entrepreneur again. I've presented my views plainly, and some people have a hard time swallowing them, especially those in the Canadian media.

I've been called "the most dangerous man in Canadian finance." My financial seminars were described in the *Globe and Mail* as "the polished staccato rhythms of a wily carny." My views on the long-term future of real estate have been a constant burr under the saddle of journalists struggling to make their mortgage payments. "What sets Turner apart," *Maclean's* magazine said in a full-page article shredding me, "is the determination with which he exhorts Canadians to borrow against their homes and invest in the market. Of course, that's why precisely client-hungry planners hire him. Many baby boomers live from paycheque to paycheque, so the only way to get them to invest heavily in funds is to push them to go even deeper into debt."

But I don't think I am the issue. The issue is risk. What most critics respond to is the notion that my strategies may be aggressive and somehow un-Canadian. We have traditionally been a nation of savers, not investors. We buy houses to live in and often to die in, not as assets to use in the wealth-building process. Canadians earn interest instead of scoring capital gains. We shun debt instead of using it as a tool. We do not seek advice about money, but quietly make our own uninformed decisions. We resent wealth and success, instead of lusting after it like the capitalists to the south. Above all, we are a suspicious people, untrusting especially when it comes to our own money. No wonder many of us have just about blown the future.

The greatest fear most Canadians have is losing their money in an investment that declines in value. That is at the heart of the opposition to a notion such as borrowing against real estate equity to invest in equity mutual funds. But it is a short-term fear, and wise investors should ignore it.

In 1997, I wrote a book about this when the TSE 300 was at the 5,000 level. A year later, in the grip of the Asian flu, with the market on a temporary downer, this was the commentary in the *Globe*'s *Report on Business Magazine*: "His 'how-can-you-lose' approach of mortgaging paid-up home to buy high-flying equity funds had buyers rushing from bookstore to bank. But converts who followed that advice a year ago have probably had trouble coping not only with a sharp drop in the value of their portfolios, but with making hefty loan payments at the same time."

Again, this comment emphasizes the short-term risk inherent in buying stocks or mutual funds, which may decline, however briefly, months later. Since then, of course, markets have gone through a lot of volatility, soaring to all-time highs in the early spring of 2000, then falling in the Nortel-influenced tech wreck of 2001, before recovering again. Where was the true risk in this? Had you followed strategies proposed in my 1995 book *2015: After the Boom*, your annual equity mutual fund return would have been more than 15%. If you sat on your real estate equity over this time, the average return in the Toronto area would have been less than 5%; in Vancouver, zero.

The immediate risk is listening to the advice and comments of people who think that what happens over six months, or a year, matters. In terms of lifetime financial planning and wealth accumulation, that is a blip. The real risk for Canadians today is not losing money but outliving their money. Face it: most people do not have indexed pensions to retire on. The average RRSP has less than $50,000 in it, and the average RRSP owner is over forty. The average annual RRSP contribution is about $5,000, which means the average Baby Boomer who has RRSPs (and a shocking number do not) will have a nest egg of less than $150,000 by the time retirement rolls around. How long will that last?

The trouble is, life expectancy is moving ever higher, and the Boomers will probably live longer than any generation that preceded them. My father died at eighty-five. At eighty-seven, my mother is still travelling—everywhere from Egypt to Newfoundland. Thank God my father bequeathed her a schoolteacher's indexed pension.

How, exactly, do most Canadians plan to finance twenty to thirty years of retirement without a retirement cache of at least half a million dollars? What happens if I am even partially right, and twenty years from now a lot of Boomers desperate for money to live on flood the real estate market with their paid-up homes, driving prices down?

Does anyone seriously expect the stock market to be lower in ten years than it is now, given the rapid pace of technological change, the paying-off of government debt, lower inflation, cheaper interest rates, global free trade and steady economic growth? Why wouldn't you invest your retirement money in the stock market, especially now that capital gains taxes have been slashed?

What is the true nature of risk today?

I often point people to a York University study that found a sixty-year-old woman who invested $500,000 in GICs, in an effort to avoid risk, would run out of money twice as fast as if she had invested in mutual funds—despite the constant fluctuations of the market.

This is the myth of risk. Determine what you really need to fear. Then face it.

The price of safety

A lot of people thought they had this risk thing licked back in the late 1990s, with the widespread introduction of segregated funds. These are insurance products masquerading as mutual funds. The idea is simple: whatever the stock market does over the next ten years, you are guaranteed that you will get all your money back. The price for this guarantee is a slightly higher management fee. However, not all the details about seg funds are positive:

- Securities regulators have expressed serious concerns about the ability of segregated fund issuers actually to make good on the guarantee, should the need arise. Therefore, the management fees have increased in many cases, and could balloon further, eroding the return investors can expect.
- If you withdraw money from a seg fund before the end of the term (typically, ten years), it can do major damage to the guarantee. The formula seg fund companies use means that if you invested $100,000 and then took out $25,000 a few years later, when the fund had grown to $125,000, your guarantee would fall back to $80,000, not to $100,000.
- Older investors may simply not qualify to buy segregated funds.
- Seg funds are generally thought to be creditor-proof, unlike RRSPs, but that can always be overturned by the courts.
- These funds provide an investment guarantee that is probably not worth the cost. Will stock markets be lower in a decade than they are now? I find that notion inconceivable. This is expensive insurance.
- However, for some risk-averse investors who want to borrow against their home equity for investment purposes, seg funds can provide peace of mind.

Should you be insured?

Of course you should, but only in the right way, and at the right cost. In some cases you have no choice but to spend money on insurance. Driving a car, in most cases, requires mandatory insurance. Be careful to reduce premiums with a high deductible amount and to fight every traffic ticket you get, lest a moving violation becomes a part of your driving record.

You also have no choice about insurance when it comes to a high-ratio mortgage. If you borrow more than 75% of the purchase price of a home (and remember, you can actually go to 95%), then the law requires you to insure it with CMHC or GE Capital. Take care in this instance that you don't make the mistake 90% of borrowers do, and just add the premium to the mortgage principal. You'd do better to put it on your credit card and pay it off over the next year. Better still, borrow it from family.

If you don't have to take mortgage insurance—if the loan is a conventional one, for less than 75% of the home's value—then don't. Mortgage insurance at the bank is outrageously expensive, and you're far better off putting the money into life insurance (see below).

Apart from these things, you need insurance on your house and what's in it. In general, residential insurance is cheap, so get as much as you possibly can. Lower the premium costs by installing a monitored security alarm system and bolt locks. In the city, the big threat is being broken into and cleaned out; in the country, it's fire. Your insurance premium will reflect the distance of your house from a fire hydrant or fire hall. Make sure you don't underestimate the value of your contents; take out added coverage for art, musical instruments and jewellery.

If you have a business, insurance is critical. Insure your premises against injury or death of employees or clients, as well as against loss through theft or fraud. Also make sure the package you arrange contains business interruption insurance, which will pay your bills if some unforeseen event shuts you down. Of course, self-employed people should also have disability insurance, which will replace lost income should you get sick or injured and be unable to run the shop.

The biggest decision, however, relates to life insurance. A 2001 survey by Finactive, the on-line division of Imperial Life Assurance, found that while almost 90% of Canadians believe life insurance is a critical part of financial planning, only 40% know anything about it. Among 18- to 34-year-olds the results were even more shocking, with just 11% professing any knowledge of what kind of life insurance to buy.

Nevertheless, when most people get married, buy a house or have a child, they feel compelled to buy insurance, which is why there are a lot of rich banks and insurance companies in Canada. I have been astonished at how many folks take out big, expensive life insurance policies that they, or their beneficiaries, stand about a zero chance of ever benefiting from.

There are only two kinds of life insurance that you need to know about.

- **Temporary insurance.** This is called "term insurance," which means you own it for a defined period of time, so long as you make the payments on it. Typically, people buy a ten-year term, with automatic renewal for subsequent terms, but at ever higher rates. As you age, you become statistically more likely to die, so the insurance cost rises.

    To get term insurance, count on filling out a detailed application form. You will then be contacted by one or two people who will grill you on various financial aspects of your life (the more insurance you want, the more questions). A medical examination will follow, including blood work, a urine sample, an electrocardiogram and various fingers stuck in various orifices. The process usually takes a couple of months from application to approval.

    Term insurance is relatively cheap, and as the banks all get into this business, it will get cheaper. You should buy it for very specific purposes, like providing a tax-free lump sum payment to your spouse or family upon your death; to pay off an outstanding mortgage or other debts; to finance your children's educations; and for funeral expenses. You should expect the insurer to offer you guaranteed premiums over the term of the insurance, regardless of changes to your age or health; renewable coverage with no medical exam or questions at the end of each term until you reach a certain age (usually eighty); and the ability to convert a term policy into a permanent one, also until a specified age (such as sixty-nine).

These days much of the approval process can be done on-line, but you still have to undress for the physical.

- **Permanent insurance.** There are three main forms: whole life, variable life and universal life. This kind of insurance is more flexible; it lasts your entire life; and it can play an integral part in lifetime financial planning, including providing tax-free retirement income.

  Whole life, like term insurance, pays you a guaranteed death benefit in return for you making premium payments that stay the same forever, regardless of age or health. The earlier you sign up, the lower the payments will be. A whole life policy also has a cash value that builds up over time, and you can borrow against that at relatively low rates, or use it to make the premium payments themselves. Whole life costs more than term insurance, and it is a truism that most people are better off "buying term and investing the difference."

  Variable life is like an insurance mutual fund. So, while the premiums you have to pay stay the same, the actual cash value of the policy fluctuates according to the performance of the assets you choose to have the policy invested in. The death benefit is guaranteed. Given the fact that you might have this kind of policy in place for ten, twenty or thirty years, hitching it to a major stock market through an index fund is probably a brilliant move.

  Universal life is divided into two parts: a basic term insurance policy, which will pay a stated death benefit so long as basic premiums are paid, and an investment account. You are allowed to put more money into this policy than is required for the basic death coverage, and that additional sum goes into a tax-free account, just like an RRSP. Within that account you can elect to invest in just about any kind of asset you want, from fixed-income bonds to high-octane index or equity growth funds.

Upon retirement, you can use all the accumulated cash inside the plan as collateral at the bank to receive a loan paying you income for the rest of your life. The most appealing aspect of this plan is that, because the money is flowing from the proceeds of a life insurance policy, the retirement income is tax-free. You can also roll it over inside your estate on a tax-advantaged basis.

For most people, term insurance is the way to go—certainly until you hit your forties and start making the best money of your life. At that point, while still in relatively good shape, convert to a universal life plan. This will retain the death benefit and yet allow you to make serious investment choices within a tax-free environment, all for relatively low basic premiums. This is especially the case for people with higher incomes, who have money left over every year after maxing out their RRSP contributions.

Caution: Be aware that the section of the Income Tax Act that allows this tax-free pension might be repealed. In fact, I'm sure it will be, since it's such a sweet deal. However, any existing insurance policies stand an excellent chance of being grandfathered. Interested? Then do it—now.

No jewel of an investment

Many people believe that jewellery is an investment. Dream on. Just check out the prices of estate jewellery and you'll quickly realize that the depreciation factor is huge. Unless there is historic significance or some unique aspect to a piece of jewellery, it will usually sell at a huge discount from its original purchase price. Even gold coins, like the Maple Leafs, sell for their gold content alone, which means you're better off with bullion itself.
• Jewellery is generally high in expense and low in liquidity.

- Do not consider it a direct investment in precious metals such as gold and silver.
- You will generally be hit with retail sales taxes on the purchase of jewellery, which you will not be able to recoup.
- Don't buy a collectible such as jewellery for any other reasons than that you like it or she won't marry you without it.

Other people's money

Life used to be simple. Before the Internet, digital television and liposuction, you pretty much knew what to do: buy what appreciates and lease what depreciates. That meant always purchasing residential real estate, because rising inflation and economic growth would surely raise its value over time. It meant leasing cars, whose value would plunge the very hour you drove it off the lot, and eventually depreciate to zero.

That's when things were simple—not necessarily better, but simple.

Today the world is a far more complex, and uncertain, place. The question of whether or not you should use other people's money to get control of assets has become equally complicated. Nowadays, some cars are manufactured so well and retain value so effectively, or even rise in price with age, that it clearly makes sense to buy them. Long-term residential real estate values may be quite uncertain, so it might be wise to rent a dwelling instead of tying up a whack of cash in something that could be worth less in a decade. These days, expensive electronic assets—computers, servers and cellphones—are among the most rapidly depreciating items ever to exist on the face of the earth. In general, they lose 50% of their value in 180 days, thanks to technological advance and economic forces.

I was clearly a fool to buy new computers in 1978 (Tandy 64K, $6,000), in 1982 (Apple Mac 128K, $4,000), in 1990 (Apple

Mac 560K, $3,800), in 1996 (IBM Aptiva $2,800) and in 1999 (IBM Thinkpad, $1,900). Today, the company of which I am CEO would never dream of cutting a cheque to buy a machine, unless for tax reasons we wanted to claim the depreciation.

But it was interesting, the last time I got a new car, to discover I'd be far better off actually buying it. Why? Because it was a dream car, a $104,000 Mercedes that retains a great deal of its value at the end of five years. To lease it with no money down would require monthly payments of $1,800, a total of $108,000 over five years, for an annual cost of $21,600. To lease with $20,000 down would drop the payments to $1,100 a month, for a five-year expenditure of $86,000, or $17,200 a year. To buy the car at the end of the lease would cost another $55,000. Therefore, it made sense to buy the Mercedes for cash and drive it for five years, then sell it for $55,000, which would put my cost at $49,000, or $9,800 a year—equal to about $800 a month. That's still an unjustifiable amount of money to spend on a car, but it's a heck of a lot less than Mercedes Benz Credit would get from me on a lease basis.

Of course, there is the issue of what that hundred grand could have given me over the five-year period if it had been used for some other purpose, like being invested in growth mutual funds. It's conceivable the cash would have grown substantially. But I still needed wheels, and $100,000 invested would not have spun off enough of a return to finance the car lease.

The same big questions hang over financing a home, given the fact that inflation is not pushing real estate values up in a universal way, and that the aging of the population will bring down demand for residential properties. Should you sit on hundreds of thousands of dollars in equity? Should you carry a giant mortgage with heavy upfront interest charges? Does it make more sense to put your cash into equity mutual funds or blue-chip stocks, while remaining a renter?

The answers usually come down to cash flow. Take the course of action that is going to maximize the amount of cash available for long-term investing in growth financial assets. That rule of thumb has to be blended in with your own desire to control things that matter in your life, whether that's the perfect home or the most extravagant automobile.

In general, leasing will give you more of that cash flow, because a rent cheque is normally less than a mortgage payment, just as a car lease payment is less than a monthly purchase price for the same vehicle. This is because, when you rent or lease, you are only paying for that portion of the value of the house or the car that you are using. There is no equity being built up in the asset. With purchase comes the obligation to pay for the entire value of the house or car with every monthly cheque.

Even so, at the end of the day (as I discovered with my car) the costs of leasing or renting something can be greater than the cost of ownership, once you are able to monetize the equity remaining in the asset. With a car, you can also combine the short-term cash flow benefits of leasing with the long-term equity advantage of ownership by negotiating an option to buy it for a set price at a predetermined time in the future. That way, if you keep the vehicle in great shape, with low kilometres, it can be worth more than the buyout price, meaning you have actually realized equity during the lease period (in which you used your cash for investment purposes).

If this sounds confusing and contradictory, you understand things well. In our complex world, assets are constantly shifting in value, and most traditional rules will be challenged and broken routinely. But here are a few pointers:

- Going forward, quite powerful personal computers will cost less than $500, at which point a purchase makes total sense.
- Cellphones should normally be free with the signing of an air time agreement.
- The price of cars will decline steadily as the vehicles themselves become far superior and residual values increase. To

lease or buy will depend on your individual circumstances. In general, if you want to hang on to a vehicle for more than three years, buy it.
- Interest rates, including mortgage rates, will drop and the cost of money will fall, making home ownership less onerous. For the next half-decade, purchasing a home is fine so long as care is taken to avoid the buildup of unproductive equity. Get it out with a tax-deductible mortgage and invest the money for growth. In the long run there is absolutely no guarantee that all real estate will increase in value, so make sure you get the right kind.

What this all boils down to is: Take other people's money when it can help your cash flow, increase the potential for gain, or get you what you otherwise could not have. Never take it when only the other guy wins.

Best dead debt

What's a mortgage? *Gage* comes from a French word meaning "hand," so in Saxon days it referred to a hand that was laid on a piece of land to secure the debt of the landholder. A "live" gage meant the lender was entitled to both rent and the produce of the land. A "dead" gage meant the debtor kept the land and whatever it produced so long as he made regular payments. The French word for "dead" is *mort*, so this kind of a debt became known as a *mortgage*.

- The best mortgage strategy is to pay it off as quickly as possible, since it is a non-deductible debt and amortizing it over twenty-five years means you'll pay back $3 for every dollar you borrow by the end of the term.
- Most lenders will allow you to increase monthly payments by up to 200%, and to make annual payments of 10% or 15% of the outstanding amount. Do that whenever possible. As well, increase the frequency of your payments, ideally from monthly to weekly.
- After you have paid down all or a portion of your mortgage, take out a new one for investment purposes. Now, the interest-only payments are all deductible from your taxable income. This is a mortgage you do not want to pay off.

Children

It's estimated that the cost of a four-year university degree will rise to about $200,000 within fifteen years. At least some of that, and maybe a lot of it, will be expected to come from you, the lucky parents. Clearly, most parents today are in no position to fork over a hundred thousand dollars and still have in place an effective retirement strategy. At the same time, governments are downloading the cost of advanced education onto students. Since they are the ultimate beneficiaries, and since tuition fees, even at advanced levels, cover only a portion of schooling costs, this makes sense. But it's a huge obstacle for families to overcome.

So the feds came up with a good thing called the RESP. The Registered Education Savings Plan is a giant incentive for you to sock away money for this distant goal. Unlike an RRSP, the money you contribute is not deductible from your taxable income. But there are still two major benefits: First, all the growth in the money you put into an RESP is tax-deferred, as with an RRSP. So, if you put the cash in the right kind of investment (like an emerging markets, or science and technology, or equity index mutual fund), the returns can be immense over ten or twenty years. Secondly, for making RESP contributions, the government will give you money. That's right—free money that you never need to pay back, so long as your child enrols in a post-secondary institution. This one aspect alone makes it imperative that all families get one of these. The grant can amount to as much as $7,200 per child.

RESPs work this way: You are allowed to contribute up to $4,000 per child per year into the plan. There is a lifetime limit of $42,000, and these contributions can be made for twenty-one years after you open the plan. The plan itself can stay alive for a total of twenty-five years, after which it must be collapsed. The money you contribute can be placed into any kind of investment you want. Of course, most people do the wrong thing and put it in GICs, thinking they cannot afford to risk this cash by investing it in growth assets like mutual funds, which sometimes go down. Ironically, because you know an RESP will be in place for a defined period of time before the money's taken out, this is the ideal vehicle for high-return, high-risk assets, which will outperform over the long haul.

Contributions can come not only from parents but also from grandparents, aunts, uncles and friends of the beneficiary child or children, and you can open a family RESP that lets you invest for all your brood in a single plan.

For doing this, the government gives you money. The Canada Education Savings Grant pays you 20% of what you contribute, to a maximum of $400 a year. So, put in $2,000 and get the maximum amount. The grant contribution room can also be carried forward, for a maximum grant of $800. So if you miss one year and contribute $4,000 the next, you'll get the full $800. This free annual money is available until the end of the year in which your child turns seventeen, and there is a lifetime limit of $7,200. As an extra bonus, the feds have decreed that any children born after 1998 have the potential to receive the maximum $7,200 grant even if their RESPs are not opened until they are older.

Now, how does the money come out of the plan after years of contributions and tax-deferred growth? Well, first do some math. You are allowed to put in a total of $42,000, and the feds will chip in a max of $7,200, for a total of almost $50,000. If that money is stuck into growth assets giving you a return of 12% annually (which should not be hard to achieve in the 2000–2020 period) for the next fifteen years, it will double every six years. That should mean an educational nest egg of close to $150,000.

When your child enrols in a qualifying school, you direct your plan administrator (typically a bank) to begin making payments to your offspring, or to the school itself to pay for tuition. The amount of the payments, and the frequency, are up to you. The RESP withdrawals are taxable in the hands of the student, who must have a social insurance number. The good news is that the child's earned income is probably minimal, which means a very low tax exposure.

Now, what happens if your loving child steals a motorcycle and thunders off to a life of crime in Mexico instead of going to Queen's? You have choices. You can name another of your children to be the new beneficiary; you can withdraw the money that you contributed, tax-free. If the money's not used for educational purposes, then the grant money has to be paid back. And the growth on the original contributions must remain inside the RESP (or else it will be subject to income tax), but it can then be transferred into your RRSP, to a maximum of $50,000 (provided you have that much RRSP room). To pull this off, the RESP must have been in place for a decade, and your child has to be twenty-one years old and not pursuing higher education.

Alimony and support

> If your relationship fails, there can be serious financial consequences. Consider the different ways the law treats alimony payments and child support payments.
> - Alimony payments (to support a former spouse) are deductible from your taxable income, provided certain conditions are met. They have to be made on a regular basis, pursuant to a signed agreement or court order. The person receiving alimony must include the money in his or her income for tax purposes.
> - Child support is different. Following serious and effective lobbying by women's rights groups, Ottawa changed the law requiring women receiving child support to include it as taxable income. The flip side is that former spouses making those payments can no longer deduct them from their taxable income (a potential incentive not to make payments). This is for agreements entered into after April 30, 1997.
> - If you are negotiating a settlement, therefore, make sure that alimony and child support payments are segregated, or else the deductibility of alimony payments could be lost.

Roadkill on Bay Street

At the height of the Nortel meltdown in the summer of 2001, the picture of a devastated investor was published on the front page of the *Globe and Mail*. It turned out to be a pilot who had lost more than $200,000 on stock in the company. The cutline under the photo said this man vowed never again to take the advice of the financial community. The implication was clear: He had been told by a broker or financial adviser to load up on this darling company during and after the time it had soared in value. The bulk of his investible net worth was dumped into Nortel, just after it had peaked at over $120 a share, and then he bought a load more when it dropped into the $60 range. By the time he made it to the front page, it was well south of $20, on its way to $11.

Anyone who bothered to read the story, however, discovered that this guy was a do-it-yourselfer. He had taken his advice not from a qualified professional but from newspaper headlines. He opened an account with a discount on-line broker and then clicked his way into a load of Nortel paper. The mistakes, of course, were classic:

- He bought at the wrong time, chasing previous gains.
- He went for the big, greedy score, instead of diversifying.
- Worst of all, he arrogantly believed he could shun advice and make his own decisions in a field where he was, at best, an amateur. In short, he deserved what he got. This is akin to a financial adviser climbing into the cockpit of an Airbus and trying to take off. The result would be the same: disaster.

Millions of Canadians made similar mistakes during the great on-line craze that swept the continent as the new millennium dawned in 2000. Outfits like TD Waterhouse, Royal Bank Action Direct and Schwab Canada could not keep up with the demand. In Markham, north of Toronto, Action Direct went from occupying one floor in a suburban office building to consuming the entire structure. On the Toronto waterfront, I toured the Schwab Canada office one day in the spring of 2000, watching row after row of new workstations being installed as the company scrambled madly to keep up with demand.

TD Waterhouse took a bad media hit for keeping desperate clients on hold for forty-five minutes or longer before they were able to execute their trades. Clients complained bitterly that they were missing opportunities, and Waterhouse boss John See did all he could to make sure an explosive expansion plan was kept on track. The entire industry railed at rules requiring every on-line trade to be approved by a broker before it was executed.

Finally, the regulator gave up. Later in 2000, the Ontario Securities Commission withdrew the so-called "Know Your Client" requirement that had ensured every trade was reviewed by a broker to make sure it was appropriate to the individual investor's goals and risk tolerance. The floodgates were now open, and the days of true cowboy capitalism were upon us—just in time for the meltdown of Nortel, the dot-com implosion and the wreck of the entire tech sector.

By the spring of 2001 the rashness of that OSC decision was clearly evident. A few billion dollars had been lost from the savings accounts and RRSPs of countless amateur investors, who now left their on-line accounts dormant. Companies like Research in Motion, Wi-Lan, Lucent, 360networks and Nortel had lost 90% or more of their value. TD Waterhouse announced it was laying off seven hundred people—some of whom had been there merely a few months, hired in a frenzy and dismissed in haste. Trading volume at every discount broker collapsed. In the U.S., the largest on-line outfit, Charles Schwab, took a 51% earnings hit. At the company's Canadian subsidiary, many of those new workstations overlooking Lake

Ontario were suddenly empty again.

It turned out to be a classic case of investor mania. The markets soared and most people missed it, so they piled on afterwards. Suddenly everyone had a hot tip, or insider information, passed on in elevators and grocery stores. With equities shooting higher, risk was ignored and greed replaced caution. Scores of investors looked for the cheapest and fastest way to get into the game, leading to the on-line revolution. On television, a popular commercial for U.S. Internet discount broker Datek showed hundreds of investors storming the New York Stock Exchange, finally breaking through the glass and swarming the trading floor like so many invaders seizing the Alamo.

When they got there, however, the easy money had already been made. Investors, like the *Globe*'s front-page pilot, who had not sought advice found they lacked diversification, held high-risk assets and had bought into companies with insane price-earnings ratios. It was bound to end badly, and it did.

There are lessons from the roadkill on Bay Street that should be remembered when markets rebound and the next sure thing comes along:

- You are always better to play the stock market through a good equity mutual fund rather than investing in equities themselves. This gives you a level of diversification you could never get using your own money.
- You should never buy individual stocks with borrowed money, especially from a margin account.
- Greed blinds. Don't be motivated by it, lest you lose your way.
- Don't take a financial action just because it's cheap. Sure, you can trade on-line inexpensively, but that's hardly a reason to do so. Get some advice from a professional.
- Invest for the long term, not just the afternoon.
- Never be an on-line warrior unless you are willing to put in

the work to fully research and understand every investment decision you make. And after you make it, face up to the results, because you have nobody else to blame. Or you can call the *Globe and Mail* and whine.

Dealing with canines

OK, so you screwed up, bought a canine of a stock and lost money. Fortunately, you still have some options to minimize the pain, thanks to the tax system.

- If your capital losses exceed your capital gains, then any excess losses can be carried back three years or forward indefinitely, and be applied against your gains in any of those years.
- For example, if you bought and sold Nortel in the current year and took a big hit, and yet made money buying and selling the same stock last year, you can carry the loss back and apply it against those gains to recover taxes using this year's income tax form.
- File form T123, *Election on Disposition of Canadian Securities*, with your personal tax return. But remember, once you file this, it is irrevocable.
- Capital gains and losses are treated differently from trading gains and losses. Trading gains are fully taxable, while trading losses can be used to offset income from other sources, like salary.

Diversify, diversify, diversify

While the technology-fuelled market bubble was inflating in 1999 and into 2000, there was one constant theme reflected on the financial pages: mutual funds are for losers. In fact, the bookstore shelves have groaned lately under the weight of volumes exhorting the "beyond mutual funds" philosophy. I hope you didn't buy any.

Mutual funds are wonderful investments, and most

Canadians should own as many fund units as they can, for as long as they can. History has proven beyond a shadow of a doubt that a well-run fund like Templeton Growth or the Trimark Fund gives outstanding returns over the long haul. Of course, some years there is growth and some years there is decline. But that's exactly why these are long-term assets, which should form the very heart of most people's non-registered portfolios and RRSP holdings.

Could it be that the beyond-fund media crowd just don't understand the basics? Let's review them.

What is a mutual fund?
(also called an investment fund)

It's a pool of money—a co-operative—in which many individual investors can add relatively small amounts of cash so that, together, they amass an amount with enough clout to achieve diversification and power. The other major advantage is that this pool is managed by a professional who, unlike the investors, spends all of his or her time making sure the fund achieves its goals. The mutual fund also looks after all the administrative and accounting details for its unitholders.

Where does a fund put its money?
There are a myriad of funds for you to choose from, each focusing on a particular type of asset. Equity funds buy publicly traded stocks, either in Canada, the U.S., Europe, Asia or a combination thereof. Emerging market funds buy equities in less-developed parts of the world. Bond funds buy corporate and government bonds. Dividend funds buy preferred shares of companies that pay dividend income. Real estate funds buy real estate assets. Balanced funds buy both stocks and bonds. Money market funds buy interest-bearing investments like government treasury bills.

Therefore, there are funds that represent no risk (money market), ones that seek to have growth with little risk (balanced), ones that pace the stock market (equity) and ones that are high-risk and high-return (emerging markets or science and technology). Most funds available in Canada are open-end funds, which means they can issue an endless number of units and buy them back from investors when they want to get out.

Do all funds operate the same way?

Absolutely not. There are four main kinds: (1) Actively managed funds are the most common, and adhere to the above description: they are pools of money managed by professionals. (2) Index funds are passively managed, which means nobody is making decisions on where to invest. Instead, these equity funds just mirror a particular stock market index, like the TSE 300, and do whatever it does. (3) ETFs are exchange-traded funds, which are similar to index funds but actually trade like stocks, so the value of the units is constantly changing. (4) Segregated funds are mutual funds with a guarantee—in effect, insurance products that will always give you back your capital at the end of a specified term (usually ten years), even if the stock market has declined. If it rises, you get the gain.

What does it cost to own a mutual fund?

That depends on the type of fund. Fees are called MERs (Management Expense Ratios) and are comprised of the money paid to the fund manager plus the costs of running the thing. Actively managed funds have fees of roughly 2% to 3% of the value of the assets, while index funds and ETFs cost far less (since management is passive). With segregated funds there is a premium to be paid for the guarantee they offer, typically an extra half-point.

Funds that have sales commissions on top of MERs are called "load" funds. The commission can be payable when you first buy the fund ("front-end load") or when you sell ("rear-end load"). Typically, most people go for the latter, which is also called a DSC (deferred sales charge) fund, because the longer you hold the investment, the lower the sales charge when you sell it. Examples are AIM, Templeton and Fidelity funds, which you would normally buy through a financial adviser or broker. Funds that have no commission are called, of course, "no-load" funds. Examples are Altamira Funds and most of the ones you buy at the banks. Some critics refer to no-load funds as no-help funds, since they are generally sold directly to the public, without the filter of an adviser who recommends them. I agree with that view. Get an adviser.

How do I get out?

Selling mutual fund units is simple and fast. Just contact your adviser or the fund company and the money will likely be in your bank account the next day. Hopefully, however, you will be quick to buy and reluctant to sell, since most mutual funds (certainly the actively managed ones) are intended as long-term holds.

Statistics show us that people who buy load funds tend to hold them far longer than those who purchase no-load funds. This is probably because of where people get their investment advice: load investors get it from their financial advisers; no-load investors get it from the newspaper.

Risk and reward

Mutual funds do not equal the stock market. There are funds available for all kinds of investors—those who are terrified at the prospect of losing any money as well as those who want to aggressively grow wealth, even when confronted with major temporary risks.

- At the low end of the risk scale are money market funds, which typically invest in government securities, like treasury bills. The rate of return is low—although still higher than a GIC—and risk is negligible.
- For those who can stomach moderate risk and wish a higher yield, mortgage funds, bond funds and REITs (real estate investment trusts) are good choices. They offer fairly predictable returns and the potential for capital gains.
- Balanced funds combine both bonds and stocks, and are a popular choice among people who want to have a foot in both camps.

- For more aggressive investors, equity funds hold the common shares of publicly traded companies. Index funds mirror whatever the market in general is doing. Sector funds reflect valuations in areas like oil and gas, high tech and resources.
- At the high end of the risk/reward scale are emerging markets funds and labour-sponsored funds. The latter invest in start-up companies and smaller ventures, with the potential for huge returns or painful flame-outs. Labour funds also offer added tax incentives, and can be explosive performers within an RRSP.

The lessons of Nortel

My dentist is a part-time comedian. He's got a routine, a demo tape and an agent. Like the rest of us, he also wants to be wealthy. He owns a new Mercedes and an RRSP chock full of Nortel stock. These days, of course, he can't afford to stop being a full-time dentist. It's no joke.

Millions of people had their wealth inflated if they bought Nortel stock on the way up. But millions more had their wealth destroyed in the post-bubble meltdown that saw this company lose 90% of its value in just a few months. It was an experience of national importance: Canada's high-tech giant, a $400-billion gorilla, accounts for 36% of the entire Toronto Stock Exchange and figures prominently in many mutual funds, personal retirement plans and even the Canada Pension Plan.

Nortel was the shining star in the emerging New Economy of the global telecom market, where spending tripled between 1998 and 2000. In those heady two years, the on-line discount brokers could not cope with all the investors wanting to sign on; business-to-business (B2B) Web sites were changing hands for hundreds of millions; high-speed Internet systems were being constructed everywhere; e-commerce and e-business mutual funds were giving triple-digit returns; and my dentist's

RRSP was mushrooming beyond belief. Companies like Nortel, Lucent, Cisco, 360networks and JDS Uniphase were involved in building the Big Pipe that would wire the entire world.

As it turned out, we were all wrong. The Big Pipe in 2001 was about 95% unused, with a huge telecom glut that saw the rapid decompression of all these companies. While technology is still the undisputed engine of the future, and while the Internet continues to be the fastest-spreading technology in the history of the world, we now have a lot more Pipe than we can fill with content people actually want. The big-spending years are over, and companies like Nortel will have to shrink dramatically just to survive.

As I write this, Nortel stock has lost about 90% off its peak value of $124 a share. It now accounts for about 5% of the TSE, and has laid off 30,000 workers. Its quarterly loss of $19.2 billion in 2001 was one of the worst corporate bloodlettings in Canadian history. And all of this comes less than nine months after its chief executive officer, John Roth, predicted sustained annual growth of more than 20%, suggesting that a gathering economic storm in the U.S. would not impact his empire.

About the time Roth made that forecast, I was standing before television cameras in Toronto's Stock Market Place, interviewing a leading mutual fund manager and analyst who predicted Nortel would achieve a new 52-week high in early 2001, and encouraged investors to buy on any signs of weakness. Anyone who watched us on TV and acted on his suggestion was, like this guy's fund owners, led to slaughter.

So, what are the lessons of Nortel? In future, how can we avoid dumping our precious after-tax investment cash in a bow-wow like this? Here are some guidelines:

- Don't trust the public statements of CEOs of publicly traded companies.

    Sadly, I have learned that it is extraordinarily easy in Canada for the management of companies to affect the value of their own stock. Pumping stock can sometimes be the chief job of the chief exec, supported by hyperactive IR (investor relations) departments and megalomaniac publicists. The news media slavishly reports every comment made by senior executives, especially when the story (the Internet explosion) and the company (Nortel Networks) are sexy.

As it turned out, John Roth was a Nortel cheerleader when he should have been a manager, determining what the collapse in telecom spending was about to do to a company that supplied it with working parts.

- Don't trust the analysts.

It happened with Bre-X. It happened again with Nortel. Too many analysts, whose comments find their way into the mass media, are the employees of brokerage companies that depend upon the underwriting business of the companies they follow. At the very least, these same companies— mostly owned by the banks—make a lot of money on the commissions investors pay to buy stocks in public companies, often based on the research they themselves turn out.

Weeks and months before the Nortel collapse, which in hindsight appears to have been so inevitable, virtually no analyst on Bay Street or Wall Street was sending up black smoke. The tech boom went bust and the hot stocks went frigid and then—then!—the analysts cut their ratings. Thanks, guys.

- Don't get your investment advice from the media. See the above.
- Diversify.

My dentist learned this one. It is far, far better to have your equity money in an equity mutual fund than in equities themselves. Individual stocks can experience gigantic fluctuations in value, and the job of a good fund manager is to limit exposure to volatility while still pursuing growth. That means having money spread across a number of sectors and companies, as well as maintaining a cash reserve.

Want to invest in technology? (You should, especially now.) Then do it through a science and technology mutual fund, not through individual stocks—unless you have enough investment cash to buy a large basket of companies and hire your own portfolio manager. The same goes for investing in the four other areas that will build your future wealth: financial services, health care, demographics and biotechnology.

There will be more Nortels. Count on it.

The gap

> Have you noticed it? The gap between rich and poor is expanding explosively. In Canada, the richest 20% have incomes seven times higher than the poorest 20%. The top 10% own more than 50% of all the wealth in the country. Since 1995, the number of Canadian millionaires has increased by 20%. And it appears the wealthy are gaining at the expense of the middle class. Why?
> - The bulk of the personal net worth of most middle-income Canadians is represented by their residential real estate. Over the last decade the average value of a home in Canada has remained virtually static, after inflation is factored in.
> - Wealthy people tend to eschew do-it-yourself financial planning strategies in favour of employing financial advisers. As a result, they are more diversified, buy and sell securities less frequently, and have much more tax-efficient portfolios.
> - A growing proportion of Canadian wealth is coming from the rising class of business owner/operators. These entrepreneurs take on more financial risk on a daily basis than any other group in society, but they also tend to build their wealth in a way salary-earners can only dream of.

How to be a market winner

Buying stocks is simple and fun. You can do it through a broker, a full-service financial adviser or an on-line discount brokerage. The cost of transactions is coming down as these investment channels compete with each other, and the level of service is going up. Even no-frills discount brokers now offer reams of information and research, while traditional brokers, like Merrill Lynch and Nesbitt Burns, provide both investment advice and the ability to buy your own securities on-line.

You can track your equity investments in many ways. The tried-and-true method is via newspaper listings, published each morning. Learn to read stock tables correctly and you'll see not only yesterday's closing value of your stock, but the volume of shares traded, the intraday high and low, the 52-week high and low prices, the stock's yield, and its price-earnings ratio. Because that's probably more information than you either need or want, the divine spirit created CNBC, which begat ROBtv and other all-financial television networks. Every day you can see what the major market movers did and watch hours of analysis on short-term trends and events. Finally, the quickest way to track your portfolio is on-line. There are scores of financial Web sites that will allow you to do so, giving real-time values for your securities. The best way, however, is to sit back and read the monthly or quarterly reports that your adviser sends you.

You can buy stocks with cash or borrowed money; both methods are commonplace. A cash account requires payment for a stock on the settlement day, which is usually three days after you put in a buy order. With a margin account your broker or adviser will loan you, typically, 70% of the cash required to buy the stock, with interest charged daily. If the stock rises, you have leveraged up your profits, since you get all the gain after investing just a third of the money. But if the stock falls, you're toast; the broker whose money you used will give you a margin call, and the loan must be repaid instantly.

You can also short sell, which means selling a stock before you own it, then buying it back later at a lower price. This you do only if you are certain a company's shares are about to drop, allowing you to profit from a declining market or stock. Not for the novice or faint of heart.

You can buy preferred or common shares in many companies. Preferreds give you a preferred position with regard to equity in the company—above common shares but below creditors. They often give you income in the form of dividends, which are tax-advantaged, as are capital gains. And preferreds are generally more stable than common shares, trading in a narrower price range.

Common shares are what investors usually buy, because when they rise in value a capital gain is realized. This is the kind of money you most want to earn, since the highest possible rate of tax on it is now just 25%, or half what you pay on the money you actually have to work for.

So, how do you know what stock to buy? Here are some guidelines:

- You are always better off having a professional, like a broker, portfolio manager or adviser, handle your equity purchases rather than an amateur (and that means you). Yes, the commissions payable may be less when you buy stock yourself, on-line, but little commission often means little help or advice. While I own a lot of stock myself, I have never bought any stocks directly, leaving those decisions to the guy who manages my discretionary account.
- Be as diversified as possible. That means owning the shares of many companies, and across several sectors of the economy. Diversification ensures that you don't put all your

eggs in one stock or industry. Obviously, this is going to take a lot of money, so if you don't have hundreds of thousands of dollars to invest in equities, you are far better off sticking to equity or index mutual funds.
- Don't chase hot tips—ever.
- Don't believe anything that's posted on an Internet chat board. There are too many pump-and-dump posters hoping you will.
- Research every purchase exhaustively if you insist on making your own decisions. Today the Internet is the primary source of material, but the major brokerage companies also turn out authoritative and useful information that you can access by opening a small account with them.
- Know what a reasonable price is. Millions of dot-com investors paid excessive amounts of money to buy stock in companies that had no earnings, only the potential for future profits. That was bound to turn out badly, and it did. The measure of the quality of a stock is the company earnings per share (EPS), determined by dividing the total earnings by the number of shares outstanding. See how it stacks up against historical numbers. To determine if the current stock price is fair, look at the price-earnings (P/E) ratio, which is published every day the stock trades. The higher it is, the greater the premium you are being forced to pay.
- Buy for the long haul. Today, volatility is the hallmark of stock markets around the world, as more and more people become active investors, as the flow of corporate and economic information gets faster, and as the global economy intertwines. Short-term investors in this environment can be destroyed trying to time the market, and yet market timing is what the media is obsessed with. Forget it. Opt instead to buy good blue-chip companies and then hold them for years, if not decades. The same strategy goes for equity and index mutual funds.
- Buy when others are selling.

Human nature isn't always our best friend. When Nortel was at $100 a share, investors were lining up to buy it. When it was at $12, they were lining up to sell. History shows that, over time, markets rise. Therefore, it makes sense to buy when they are down, increasing the potential for a capital gain. In a declining market, good companies are usually punished equally with lousy ones, so buy the dips.

- Consider an index or exchange-traded fund. These mutual funds pace the broad market, allowing you to diversify across all sectors. The funds are not actively managed, have exceptionally low management fees and are tax-friendly, since there are few transactions and therefore little in the way of capital gains triggered annually. However, they are just as volatile as the market itself, which means they are for long-term investors and those who are not likely to panic and sell just when things have bottomed.

There is serious money to be made in the equity markets over the next decade, thanks to the heady mix of demographics, government finances, low inflation, falling interest rates and taxes, and technological advance. I have no doubt that major indices will double, or triple, over this period of time. But I also believe we will see more sustained volatility than ever before, with more danger for those who buy the wrong stock at the wrong time, sell for the wrong reasons, listen to the wrong advice or fail to diversify or seek wise counsel.

Three classes

"Asset allocation" is a phrase you will hear a lot when working with a financial adviser, and for good reason. There are just three kinds of assets: cash (or cash equivalents like GICs and CSBs), stocks and bonds. The key is having the right amount of your wealth in the right asset class at the right time.
- More than 90% of historical rates of return have been due to asset allocation, with less than 10% as a result of the actual investments selected.

- In a time of low inflation and low interest rates, equities generally outperform the other classes.
- Different assets attract different levels of tax. After the 2000 federal changes, capital gains are the least taxed (favouring stocks and equity mutual funds), followed by dividend income (preferred shares and dividend funds), with bonds and cash equivalents (paying interest) the most taxed.
- You must earn over $5 in interest to equal the after-tax return you'd get with $4 of dividend income or just over $2 in capital gains.

Make that mortgage tax-deductible

Imagine what it would be like if you were able, like the Yanks, to deduct all the interest on your mortgage payments from your taxable income. Since most of your payment consists of interest, that would be a windfall which would increase your wealth by slashing your tax bill.

Well, stop dreaming. You can do it. The key lies in this fundamental principle: if you borrow money to create more money, then the interest on the loan is tax-deductible. That is the logic behind General Motors borrowing millions to build a new factory; the interest is a legitimate business expense and can be used to reduce profitability, and hence taxes. Ditto for you. Borrow money to invest in the economy and receive growth on it, and the interest is a legitimate expense in your hands.

Now, there's a lot of controversy and confusion over this point, and in my opinion the blame for the obfuscation appears to lie squarely on the head of the Canada Customs and Revenue Agency, formerly known as Revenue Canada. The CCRA has failed to amend wording in its annual tax guide that is totally misleading. Here it is, under the heading "Carrying Charges and Interest Expense—line 221": "You can claim the following carrying charges and interest you paid to earn income from investments: most interest you pay on money you borrow, but generally only as long as you use it to earn investment income, including interest and dividends. However, if the only earnings your investment can produce are capital gains, you cannot claim the interest you paid."

Sadly, that little exercise in jargon has scared a lot of people away from borrowing for investment purposes, believing that if they buy stocks or mutual funds which do not pay interest or dividends, the interest on the loan is not deductible. But it is. Any financial adviser, tax lawyer or accountant will set you straight.

Equally wrong is the warning contained in some tax preparation software packages on the market, which say: "If you borrowed money to invest in stocks or mutual funds that do not earn interest or dividend income, you cannot deduct the interest you paid on your loan." That is an incorrect interpretation of CCRA's badly worded statement. Ignore it. Better still, throw out the software and let a professional do your taxes. Write this on a piece of paper and tape it to the fridge: *Interest on money borrowed to invest is tax-deductible*. End of story.

Now, on to your mortgage. There are two strategies I like for creating a tax-deductible mortgage.

Asset swap

If you have an existing mortgage on your house, you can make all or part of it tax-deductible through an asset swap. Now, most people who have mortgages also have various forms of investments, like mutual funds. The idea is to take these assets and swap them for mortgage debt. Do it this way:

1. Sell your investment assets. Cash them in, being mindful there will be a small tax bill to pay on any capital gains you realize.
2. Use this cash to pay off your residential mortgage (or a portion of it).

3. Arrange a new mortgage.
4. Use the new mortgage money to buy back the investment assets you originally sold.

Now you still own the same amount of investment assets and you still have a mortgage on your home. But because you borrowed against your home (in the form of a mortgage) in order to buy assets that create wealth, the interest on your mortgage is now tax-deductible. You have just given yourself a giant tax break.

Home equity loan

If you live in a house with no mortgage, it's even easier to build wealth and still get a fat tax reduction, using a home equity loan.

This thing is getting more common all the time, as the major lenders create products that allow you to tap into all those mortgage payments you made over the last few decades. You can generally borrow up to 75% of the appraised value of your home with an equity loan. The good news is that because the loan is well secured by the real estate, you can get it at a rock-bottom rate of interest, generally the prime rate. Even better news: so long as the money is used for investment purposes to create wealth (which you'll be taxed on later), the interest can be written off.

To make this simple and effective, most lenders will allow you to have interest-only payments, which means you never actually pay back the principal amount borrowed. But why would you want to, when the entire cost to you is deductible from your personal taxable income? So, instead of having a house with no mortgage, you end up with an investment portfolio that could be worth tens, or hundreds, of thousands of dollars, plus the ability to substantially reduce your taxable income.

But, but, but, the critics cry, by setting up a home equity loan, you have to make monthly payments on the debt, for which (even though the payments are tax-deductible) you still require a cash flow. Where's that money going to come from?

Patience. All will be revealed in the next chapter.

An RRSP mortgage

> Here's another strategy to consider: put a mortgage on your home inside your own RRSP. That way, you end up making mortgage payments to yourself. It amounts to a regular, forced transfer of wealth from your income into your tax-deferred retirement plan.
> - To accomplish this, you need an amount of cash in your RRSP sufficient to pay off an existing mortgage on your home.
> - The mortgage has to be written at a rate of interest comparable to market rates.
> - Your RRSP has to be self-directed, and you'll need the help of a financial adviser to set it up. In addition, the mortgage must be insured and administered by a third-party financial institution.
> - This is not a trick to get a cheap mortgage or to make home ownership more affordable. Rather, it's an RRSP-building strategy, the idea being to squeeze as much of your income as possible into your retirement plan while giving you a stable asset (the mortgage on your home) to hold.

Is there such a thing as good debt?

You bet there is. It's debt you never want to repay because it's of such benefit while it remains in place.

This is the case with a home equity loan, described in the last chapter. To recap, a HELOC (home equity line of credit, as you will hear many financial advisers call it) is a loan taken against the wealth you have accumulated within your residential real estate. Year after year, you have faithfully made all those mortgage payments, and with each one a little more equity has been shoved to your side of the balance sheet. Many folks thus reach their forties or fifties and suddenly have the bulk of their net worth tied up in a single asset—their homes. To me this is a dangerous and unstable situation to maintain.

While there are legions of people who cling to the notion that a physical asset like a home is a safe place to keep your wealth, I remain steadfast in the opposite belief. Real estate values have generally held firm over the last five years, in most markets, because of a relatively strong economy; and over the next five years this will likely remain the case. But one of the reasons housing will retain its value in the short term is also the seed of its eventual decline, and that is the aging of the population.

Canada has the largest proportion of Baby Boomers in the world—a legion of nine million people just entering their peak income years, who have been raised their entire lives as real-estate believers. They watched their parents grow wealth primarily through the appreciation of residential real estate values, as did I. In fact my parents had virtually no other form of investment. Luckily for them, they owned real estate during those years when rapid economic growth and runaway inflation goosed home prices as never before in history.

Today, enough of these generally affluent Boomer children are moving up into trophy homes to influence the entire market. It's the B-generation's last hurrah, after moving real estate values sharply higher in the 1980s, when they were forming families. It's also the last hurrah for housing as an appreciating asset.

Ten years from now, the average Boomer will be sixty years old and downsizing. Those big houses, especially in the suburbs, will be falling in value as demand disappears. More in favour will be smaller bungalows, townhomes and condos in near-city locations, recreational property, and adult communities on golf courses. In general, the value of residential real estate will go down, not up. You best get used to the idea now. In fact, I maintain you have five years or less to unload the kinds of houses that could turn into wealth traps before the end of the decade.

The second reason I want you to sell that big house is inflation. It's dead, gone and buried. The core inflation rate in Canada is well within the 1% to 3% range set by the Bank of Canada, even despite frequent surges in the cost of energy. As technology races along, fuelling productivity and dropping costs, inflation will be the last thing on economists' minds. On the contrary, they will be struggling to deal with deflation, when prices (and wages) fall rather than rise. Check out recent trends in the prices of cars, computers and every other electronic device. The thousands I paid for a laser printer in 1999 would now be mere hundreds. The printer is a doorstop. It deflated to nothing. I thought of that the other day as I walked down Bay Street and saw some video monitors and an electronic typewriter sitting on the curb amid garbage bags.

For my parents, inflation was good. My father's salary (and the pension based upon it) went up every year. The value of their home rose relentlessly, as did their net worth. It produced a great outcome in retirement: indexed pension and cash from the sale of a house that tripled in price every half-decade. But those days are vanishing quickly, and as demand for large homes dries up, there will be no environment of generally rising prices to sustain the value of the asset.

So, think hard about whether you want to keep your equity in your home or get it out now, while real estate is still a viable commodity. Think hard about the long-term wisdom of a home equity loan, which I consider to be good debt.

If you borrow to invest in growth assets, like stocks or mutual funds, the interest is tax-deductible. You get a significant tax break at the same time as your equity is being put into things that will mushroom in value over the coming years. But how do you cope with the cash-flow demands of having a home equity loan in place? After all, you need to make interest-only monthly payments.

The answer is a SWP (pronounced *swip*), or systematic withdrawal plan, and here is how it works. With the help of a financial adviser, arrange a home equity loan in the form of a line of credit, with interest-only monthly payments (you should avoid taking this money in the form of a mortgage, with blended payments of both interest and principal). Your payments are now entirely deductible from taxable income, so long as you put the money in the right place.

Use the funds to buy units in equity mutual funds. (Some people feel more comfortable with segregated funds, since they want a guarantee against loss. However, higher fees will impair fund performance.) Have your adviser set up a SWP, which means enough money can be taken from the fund on a systematic, monthly basis to cover off the interest-only payment on the home equity loan. Now it is the mutual fund that is making the loan payments rather than you. But every year, when you fill out your tax return, the interest is deductible in your hands!

Held long enough (a minimum of five years), the mutual fund should give you substantial capital growth, despite the fact that you have removed money through the SWP to cover all financing charges. It's a win-win situation: the HELOC is good debt and the SWP is a great way to finance it.

But what if you borrow against your home and buy mutual funds that decline in value? This is a question media critics often toss out, but it doesn't have much validity. Unless history is no guide, mutual funds based on the performance of companies that are part of the economy increase in value over the long haul. Of course, there are years when markets decline, but they are far outnumbered by years of gains. So you may well buy assets with a HELOC that temporarily fall in value; but because your loan is secured by the value of your home and not by the value of the funds you buy, there will never be a margin call to make up the shortfall (as is the case with borrowing money to buy stocks from a broker). Meanwhile, of course, you continue to write off the interest on the loan against your taxable income, for a net benefit.

Finally, you will never incur a loss on funds that have gone down in value unless you take the wrong advice and sell. The proper strategy is to wait out any market correction and ignore those who confuse short-term events with long-term trends. They know not what they do.

The last resort

> The rules allow you to withdraw money from your RRSP to buy a home. An individual can take up to $20,000 and a couple up to $40,000 for a down payment. The money is, in effect, an interest-free and tax-free loan from your RRSP. It is even possible to increase the size of your down payment using the RRSP rules: make sure an RRSP contribution is made ninety days prior to the Home Buyers' Plan withdrawal and you will get a tax refund to add to the loan.
>
> However, I don't think raiding your RRSP is a good idea. Here's why:
> - Over the next decade or so, I am sure that financial assets (like stocks, bonds and funds) will grow in value more quickly than residential real estate. Your wealth will be higher if you can leave the RRSP investment intact.
> - In fact, if you withdrew $5,000 from your RRSP and didn't repay it for thirty years, assuming a 10% rate of return, you'd have $85,000 less in retirement.
> - If there is anywhere else you can get the money for a down payment, go there first. Go to your RRSP last.

The only way to earn money

I guess it was a shameless piece of electioneering, but who cares? It was the right thing to do. With only a few days remaining before the October 2000 federal election, Paul Martin, the finance minister, brought in immediate changes that dropped the capital gains tax inclusion rate dramatically. As a result, you are allowed to keep, tax-free, 50% of any capital gain that you earn—through the profit on the sale of an apartment building, a stock, a small business, a mutual fund or any other capital asset. It was a welcome move and marked the second time in just nine months that the federal Liberals sliced the tax on such gains.

This was hugely significant, because it represented a sea change for these guys. It was the Liberals, after all, who ended the $100,000 lifetime capital gains exemption, and who increased the tax rate from 50% to 75%. Their thinking was that only the well-off in society dabble in investments that earn capital gains, and so are fair game for tax increases. This is in sharp contrast to what's happened in the United States, where capital gains are taxed very favourably. In fact, in that country, taxes on gains are reduced the longer you own an asset.

But now the fundamental logic of make-the-rich-pay has been questioned in Canada, as it should be. The ability to make a profit from an investment, and to keep a fair amount of it in your pocket, is an essential building block of capitalism. It's what defines our society as one that's driven by the entrepreneurial spirit—where people take risks, start businesses, create jobs and buy into other people's enterprises. This is recognition that entrepreneurs and investors should not be taxed in the same way as savers or employees, because they create wealth and expand the economy, instead of just hoarding their wealth and collecting interest or clipping coupons. In fact, the worst way to earn income now is in the form of interest or a salary, and the best is capital gains. So, ditch those GICs, CSBs, money market mutual funds and savings accounts, and load up on equities and funds—regardless of what tax bracket you may be in.

A reader of my syndicated newspaper column recently criticized me for using as an example someone in the 50% tax bracket to illustrate the effect of this wonderful, enlightened tax cut:

> I disagree that "most middle-class people" earn upwards of $60,000, the point at which the highest federal rate kicks in. My wife and I gross about $110,000 between the two of us, and I consider us very solidly middle-class. I realize that by using the highest rate, it packs more punch and makes the point more strongly (or at least more dramatically). However, I feel that as the Baby Boomers begin to retire (and begin living on $30,000 to $40,000 yearly), more attention should be paid to middle-income people when discussing financial matters and strategies.

It's a good point. In fact, the average family income today of about $54,000 could take a big trip south as more people now in their fifties do retire on modest investment incomes, many of them house-rich and very cash-poor.

However, when it comes to keeping more of your capital gains on investments, the news is even better for families in the lower tax brackets. That's because under the new rules you get to keep half of your gain, while paying tax on the other half at your own marginal rate. So, for someone in the 50% tax bracket, the effective overall tax rate on capital gains drops to 25%. If you are in the 30% tax bracket, half the capital gain would be free and the other half taxed at your own marginal rate. So if you earned a gain of $1,000, then $500 would attract no tax and the other $500 would attract $150 in tax, for an overall capital gains tax rate of just 15%. Not bad: keep 85% of your gain! That is still twice as good a deal as you'd get on an equivalent amount of interest income (or pension or salary income).

In the future, making money via capital gains will only get better. The Americans are mulling more cuts. The federal Conservatives' last platform called for the elimination of capital gains taxes in Canada. Paul Martin has made it clear that he understands cutting capital gains taxes further is a relatively cheap and very effective way of channelling more money into the economy for job creation and business expansion.

For investors, it should be a no-brainer: invest in equity mutual funds and keep 75% of the return, or invest in GICs or money market funds and keep only 50% of what your investment generates. In fact, the tax on capital gains is now slightly less than the rate on dividend income.

Of course, people who like paying tax should earn most of their income in the form of a salary, take their retirement income in the form of a pension, and put their investment cash into safe, interest-bearing things like guaranteed investment certificates and savings bonds. Just like most Canadians. Pity.

The rule of 72

> The rule of 72 is useful to remember. Take 72 and divide it by the rate of return an investment is giving you; the result is the number of years it will take for your money to double. For example, a GIC or cash account paying 4% will double your money every thirteen years, while an equity fund giving you an average of 12% will double it in six years. The results are most pronounced within the tax-free atmosphere of an RRSP.
> - If you are thirty-two years old and put $4,300 into an RRSP every year until you are sixty-five, and it earns an average of 8%, you will have $600,000 in retirement.
> - If you start doing the same thing at age twenty, you will retire with $1.5 million.

The burden of wealth

A million bucks isn't what it used to be, but whenever the media refers to a person as a "millionaire," it's meant as an elitist, and usually negative, term—at least in Canada. In the States it's a different thing, as self-made, egocentric rich people like Ted Turner and Donald Trump are sources of both envy and pride. In the U.S., wealth means success in a capitalist society. Here, it means you probably won by shafting other people, and you should feel guilty.

Nevertheless, the number of millionaires in Canada is growing quickly, increasing by more than 40% over the last five years. At the end of 2000 there were 315,000 Canadians with $1 million or more, up from 225,000 in 1996. A bunch of that money was made in the bull market of the second half of the 1990s, and a bunch more came from inheritances. In any case, by the end of the decade we are now in, management consulting firm Cap Gemini Ernst & Young Canada figures there will be about 900,000 millionaires.

Of course, that's not nearly enough. In 2010 the average Baby Boomer will be sixty years old. There are nine million Boomers in Canada, which means that if every single millionaire was a Boomer, then nine out of ten Boomers would not be millionaires. At sixty, each person in this demographic group will have a very good chance of living another thirty years, which, at a modest $50,000 per year (even minimal inflation over the next forty years would make that a paltry amount), would chew through $1.5 million. In other words, pensionless Boomers with a million dollars by 2010 could be in for a less than enjoyable retirement.

There are two challenges here. The first is getting the million bucks into your hands—into your RRSP, your bank account and your portfolio of stocks, bonds and mutual funds. (Remember that you do not want the bulk of your net worth in real estate, because it is illiquid and cannot easily give you what you will really need, which is income.) You *can* achieve that wealth. Invest in growth assets for the long haul, get professional help, take income in tax-advantaged forms, don't wander blindly into too many RRSPs, deal correctly with volatility, understand the true nature of risk, borrow the right way, and diversify.

The second challenge is keeping wealth once you have it. This sounds a lot simpler than it really is. It takes an immense amount of work, since there are many risks to your money. The biggest risk is taxation, as the Canadian system is unfairly biased against wealthy people (we should be encouraging the accumulation of money, not punishing it, since the coming demographic crisis will overwhelm government). Other risks include an ill-conceived investment strategy, attempts to time the market, inappropriate advice and sheer stupidity. I have been amazed at the number of wealthy people I've seen (usually doctors, for some reason) who put heaps of money into investments simply because they provided tax relief. In many cases that was all they gave, as the investment itself crumbled.

Mutual funds, well chosen, provide a viable way to preserve and build wealth in a relatively risk-free way. Another way is managed money. This is a huge growth industry these days, as the number of wealthy people rises. Assets available for managing are expected to rise from $1.7 trillion in 2000 to a stunning $4.2 trillion by 2010. Companies like BMO Harris Private Banking, a division of the Bank of Montreal, along with Assante, Merrill Lynch and RBC Financial Group, are positioning themselves as one-stop resources for folks with sizable investible assets.

"Managed money" is a term you hear a lot, and the definition varies from company to company. In general it involves turning over basic investment decisions to a professional money manager. It also means you get to access a level of expertise once available only to those with vast assets. Today, for example, several brokerage houses offer managed money programs to clients with as little as $100,000. That money is serviced by managers who normally would deal only with clients who had ten or twenty times that wealth.

If you get into a managed money program, here's what you should expect:

- One all-inclusive fee based on the size of your portfolio, not on the number of transactions. This encourages proper

money management, not churning. The fee is also tax-deductible, unlike mutual fund fees.
- No additional charge for custodial services for your securities or for trades.
- Extensive reporting—usually a monthly statement plus a detailed quarterly review that assesses current asset allocation and analyzes portfolio performance; also, an annual reporting package giving all information required for tax filing, including portfolio transactions, capital gains and losses, deposits and transfers.
- The services of a portfolio manager, who also acts as a personal financial consultant or has the ability to assemble a team of experts to deal with every financial aspect of your life.

Now, jumping into a managed money program takes some confidence. For starters, you have to sign documents giving discretionary management of your money to someone else. That means another person will be deciding what assets to buy and sell, in what quantities and at what time. All you will do initially is determine the general parameters of your portfolio based on your risk profile and investment objectives—what percentage of your wealth will be in equities, bonds and cash, for example. After that, you will just have to trust how much Nortel or Canadian Pacific is being bought with your hard-earned money.

As scary a leap as that sounds, it is worth taking. I know from experience, having given over all my investible assets to a professional portfolio manager several years ago. Now he not only makes fundamental investment decisions but also pays quarterly taxes, finds money when I need it to do something strange with, works with my accountant, and provides me with advice on everything from corporate affairs to insurance. As a result, my portfolio sailed through the tech wreck of 2000–2001 unscathed, and I was spared the burden of making active investment decisions. Instead, I concentrated on making more money instead of worrying about losing it. What a blessing that was.

Yes, you can

> Always remember that you can write off the interest payments on money you borrow to make more money. But the rules on this point are not crystal clear, or well understood, thanks in part to murky wording by Canada Customs and Revenue Agency and misinterpretation by many so-called tax experts.
> - To claim the interest as an expense, you must invest in assets that pay you a return greater than the interest you pay to rent the money.
> - Yes, interest on money borrowed to buy stocks and mutual funds *is* deductible from your taxable income, whether or not you receive any dividends or capital distributions. Fie on anyone who tells you otherwise.
> - Interest on money borrowed to buy assets for your RRSP is no longer deductible.
> - If you borrow to buy an asset that declines in value, the interest is deductible even after you sell the asset if you use the proceeds to pay down debt or buy another asset.
> - Most lenders will allow you to borrow and make interest-only payments, which means that 100% of your outflowing cash is a tax write-off.

Don't beat the Street

Don't even try. The stock market is a self-regulating god, perfect in its random, short-term unpredictability. It will do what it will do, reacting to events nobody can predict and trends you are powerless to influence. The market is made up of millions of human minds all trying to understand what to do next. Picture a school of trout, countless of them, swimming just before you in the clear stream. As you stride through the water in your hip waders, the school turns this way, then that, a single entity, yet teeming with division. Almost always the school chooses rightly and avoids danger, but some fish end up darting the other way, into your net. Others find the deepest, coolest places.

There are two kinds of investment approaches, active and passive. Active investors try to beat the Street. They get all the attention, the press and the glory when they're right. They are people like Peter Lynch of Fidelity, Mark Mobius of Templeton and Ian Ainsworth of Altamira—mutual fund managers who have achieved star status because they actively sought out companies that gave their funds returns vastly exceeding the market averages.

This star factor has permeated our investment culture. All the newspapers and financial magazines rate mutual funds every month or every quarter, ranking them by their short-term performance. Financial newspapers like the *Globe*'s *Report on Business* keep track of the week's "stars" and "dogs" in terms of funds and individual equities. Companies like Morningstar publish detailed rankings of major funds in Canada and the U.S., ascribing so many stars to each. Financial Web sites like StockHouse contain chat boards where tens of thousands of investors swap the latest hot tips, gossip, advice and rumours on where to invest to catch the Next Big Thing.

Active investors are divided into two groups, those who seek growth and those who seek value.

- Growth investors try to spot companies on the move, which offer the potential for quick capital gains as other investors realize the potential and pile on. Their targets are companies with rapid growth rates, even if profits are lagging behind or non-existent. More important for them is the potential for earnings, and for a rise in the stock value as that potential is realized. Classic examples of these investments were the Internet and dot-com stocks that investors couldn't get

enough of in the late 1990s—often companies with just an idea but no track record, no expectation of profit, who lived off the money the market threw at them. While that tech bubble ended in collapse, growth investors who bought in at an early stage and sold at the zenith made huge amounts of money.
- Value investors want nothing to do with hype, potential for future success or rapid capital gains. Instead, they actively seek out companies that are undervalued, selling at market values below the actual value of the assets they own. The formulas used to identify such stocks include price-to-earnings ratios and price-to-sales ratios, along with the corporate balance sheet. Value investors are willing to wait for their returns, and choose a path of less risk to get there. For the first half of the 1990s, as markets were choppy and uncertain, value funds like Trimark were hugely in favour. During the second half of that decade, when tech stocks were the rage, so were growth funds like Altamira's Science and Technology.

The trouble with most active investing, for either growth or value, is that it doesn't work. That is to say, eight times out of ten, actively managed mutual funds fail to beat the Street. History shows us that 80% of the time over the last fifteen years, you would have been better off to have your money stashed in an index fund that passively mirrored whatever the market itself was doing.

In general, indexing is a winning strategy, so long as you don't try to time the market. It is better to give up any hope of outperforming the market in the security that you will never underperform it. That realization, combined with the incredible volatility of markets over the last few years, has led to a massive increase in the size and number of index funds. In Canada now, all the major banks offer a squadron of index funds, with CIBC remaining the leader.

Indexing works because, by keeping investors buried inside the school of trout, it avoids the sudden decisions that rogue fish take, either rightly or wrongly. Buying an index fund means you are tying your fortunes to the largest companies ("large capitalization" or "large-cap" stocks) that make up an index like the TSE 300, Standard & Poor's 500 or the Dow Industrials. So long as you commit to owning an index fund for long enough (a minimum of five years), you will ride out the temporary volatility on the market's steady march to a higher place.

But why does passive investing almost always beat active investing? After all, it shouldn't be that way. Smart people who can track things like economic trends, demographics, the course of interest rates and technological advance should be able to pick sectors and market-leading companies whose growth will be greater than that of the general economy, as measured by the Dow or the TSE. That, after all, is what you pay management fees to mutual fund managers to figure out.

The reason is simple. It's human nature. Active investors, even the professional fund managers, are by definition trying to get ahead by making temporary decisions. That opens the door for ego and emotion to cloud the decision-making process; for a hot tip to replace research; and for strategic inconsistency as investors try to react to every interest rate adjustment, trade figure or tax change. The victim here is perspective and the long view.

When active investing seizes the attention of the media, then everybody wants to own the same companies—the ones with the star stock performances that have usually led them to be worth much more than the assets behind them, and that have shot skyward in terms of price-to-earnings ratios. Remember: many active investors lined up to buy Nortel at $100 and then lined up to sell it at $12. These investors in this and other hot technology companies lost more than 80% of their money, while passive investors who may have bought an index fund on the day Nortel was at its absolute peak were down little more than 30% at its absolute trough.

If you can strip human fear, greed and hope out of active investing, then expect to win. If you can't, don't even try. But there is no excuse for everyone not having a profound exposure to the market, judiciously purchased and long held.

Don't have creditors

> There is no law preventing creditors from going after what's in your RRSP—a fact that shocks most people. Be aware that your retirement nest egg could be at risk in several ways. For example:
> - If your marriage breaks up, your spouse can make a claim against your RRSP and chances are you will lose half of everything.
> - If you die and owe the government money, your RRSP can be opened subject to the Income Tax Act, for repayment of those back taxes plus accrued interest and penalties.
> - If you go bankrupt, creditors can get a court order against your RRSP.
> - If the financial institution holding your plan goes down, you could lose all your assets beyond the insured limit of $60,000 for guaranteed assets like GICs and cash. There is no coverage for mutual funds.
> - Segregated funds are more creditor-proof but still subject to being broken into if a court determines you put money in there just to escape your creditors.
> - The best advice: don't have creditors.

Dollarization

In the 1950s, one Canadian dollar was worth more than an American dollar by about a dime. In the late fifties, Prime Minister John Diefenbaker pegged the dollar at just over 90 cents U.S., sparking national outrage and contributing to his eventual political defeat.

These days, the dollar routinely plunges into the 60-cent

U.S. range, making travel in the States a personal financial nightmare, delighting our exporters, raising import prices and creating disputes as American business people accuse us of unfair trade practices. The low dollar is controversial, and things could well get a lot louder in the years to come. According to CIBC economist Jeff Rubin, "In another five or six years we'll have a five-handle on the currency. People are going to ask themselves, what's the benefit of having a national currency if it just makes us poorer?"

It used to be that the impact of the weak Canadian dollar for travellers to the States was offset by lower American prices. But today that's gone. A $5 meal at McDonald's in Winnipeg will cost you $5 U.S. in Duluth, which can equal seven loonies and two quarters. The slide in the value of Canadian money against the greenback has been relentless now for a generation, and while some people argue that all major currencies have given up ground against the American one, only Canada has virtual economic integration with the elephant to the south.

Why wouldn't we end the charade, the exchange rate volatility and the costs of a national currency, and adopt the U.S. dollar? I believe we will, and every thinking investor should be getting ready for dollarization.

Of course, we all know the arguments against giving up the Canadian currency. As Southam columnist and nationalist Susan Riley has written, "Giving up the loonie would be a profound symbolic retreat, the most graphic evidence yet of how much sovereignty we have sacrificed for free trade. It could mean the end of Canada as an independent country."

There are valid arguments against dollarization. For example, the Bank of Canada would be irrelevant and unnecessary, since fiscal and monetary policy would be set in Washington by the Federal Reserve. That means inflation targets and interest rates would come out of the Fed. However, any rate change in the States today is certain to be copied here, lest our financial markets get out of sync with the American ones.

The pro-loonie forces also argue that our existing floating exchange rate system helps to buffer the shock of volatile commodity prices, which are usually expressed in U.S. dollars. But this is becoming less and less a factor as our old commodity-based economy becomes increasingly rooted in technology, manufacturing and knowledge-based industries.

Then there is the reality that a low Canadian dollar translates into cheap exports, which can undercut American competitors who have to price their wares in greenbacks. Absolutely true, but this artificial competitive advantage has given rise to the justified American defence that Canada's deliberate cheap-dollar policies constitute an unfair trade practice under the North America Free Trade Agreement (NAFTA).

Finally, there is the emotional, historical and political position that no country without a national currency is actually a country, just a territory of the United States. That was argued in places like Ecuador and Peru before they dollarized, but the argument was ultimately defeated.

So what benefits would there be to Canada and Canadians if we adopted the American dollar? First and foremost, it could significantly increase trade between Canada and the States—trade that's at the very heart of our ongoing ability to live beyond our means. Without trade, our small domestic population could never afford the array of social programs that exist today. "Dollarization may contribute to trade integration with the United States to an extent that would not be possible otherwise," according to International Monetary Fund economists Andrew Berg and Eduardo Borensztein. "The volume of trade among Canadian provinces is more than twenty times that of their trade with U.S. states ... The use of a common currency may be an important factor in explaining this pattern of national market integration, given the fairly low transaction costs and restrictions to trade across the Canadian–U.S. border." In other words, anywhere that trade can be conducted in the same currency, the odds of an exponential increase are real.

Dollarization would simply make free trade work harder, and likely attract a lot more foreign investment to a Canadian economy even more integrated with the American one. It would end today's currency volatility, giving business what it always wants: predictability. By eliminating currency risks, dollarization could end up reducing interest rates, and thus the cost of everyone's mortgage and business loan. As the IMF points out, "An expected benefit from the elimination of the risk of devaluation would be the reduction of country risk premiums, and thus lower interest rates, which would result in a lower cost of servicing the public debt and also in increased investment and faster economic growth."

Naturally, operating in U.S. dollars would lower the cost of American imports, which is a big factor for companies buying American high-tech equipment, or indeed for anyone who likes oranges or fresh greens during the Canadian winter. Finally, dollarization would give us something we have not enjoyed in decades: confidence in the currency.

And let's face it, what lies behind paper money today? Not gold. Not real estate or any physical assets. Only confidence. Paper money is not a product but a promissory note, to be exchanged for something else. The money you work for has no value of its own, but can be turned into commodities you need or want—shelter, food or a DVD player.

So long as Ottawa allows a low-dollar policy to continue, your wealth is being eroded against the one global standard that exists. Our foreign debt becomes more difficult and more expensive to repay. Our interest rates are higher than they need be, and we have created an impediment to free trade. Why are an increasing number of Canadian companies operating in American dollars? Simply because they can see the writing on the wall, through all the smoky rhetoric and emotional posturing that dollarization will give rise to over the next five to seven years, until it becomes absolutely clear there is no alternative. Astute investors should see it too, and be converting into U.S. dollars before the ratio of $1.50 Canadian to $1 American becomes two to one, then three to one. U.S. dollar investment accounts, U.S.-pay bonds and preferred shares, and American and international equity funds are all ways of preparing today for tomorrow.

Newfoundland too once had its own proud currency.

Our exit tax

> Does Canada have an exit tax? In effect, it does. That means if you choose to leave Canada and emigrate to another country, such as the United States, there are tax consequences. On the day of departure you are deemed to have disposed of all property for proceeds equal to fair market value, with these exceptions:
> - Real estate located in Canada.
> - Assets used in operating a business permanently located here.
> - Pension assets, like RRSPs and RRIFs.
> - Stock options.
>
> If the value of other assets you own when you stop being a Canadian resident exceeds $25,000, then you must report the total value and details. If you leave, you are no longer taxed in Canada on income earned elsewhere, but you will still be dinged for Canadian-sourced income even though you are a non-resident. The withholding rate on interest, dividends and pension income is 25%.

How to find an adviser you can trust

Of the hundred or so e-mails I receive every day from people I've never met, a shocking number start something like this: "I have an investment adviser that I am not happy with" or "I've been burned, and now just can't trust any investment companies."

A lot of people seem to have unrealistic expectations about what a financial adviser can do for them. Some want double-digit returns year after year after year. Others want immediate results, within weeks of signing up with an adviser. And still others are furious when they have to pay more tax than anticipated on an inheritance or investment income. But many people do receive bad advice from incompetent folks passing themselves off as qualified financial advisers. You should be aware that in most of Canada (the notable exception being Quebec) there are absolutely no laws governing who may, or may not, call himself or herself an adviser. That has led to the sorry situation in which every sales rep out flogging life insurance products, limited partnerships, real estate deals or mutual funds can hang out the shingle of a financial adviser.

Obviously, in a country where plumbers, mechanics and dermatologists are licensed and registered, this is a serious omission. The lack of regulatory standards has caused a lot of heartbreak and lost fortunes, and the feds should work towards the establishment of minimum standards. This was reinforced for me recently as I waited to start a financial seminar. As the large crowd settled into their seats, an elderly woman came forward and hesitantly handed me an envelope. She left without speaking. When I read it, I was shocked at her story. At the age of seventy-one she had entrusted all her wealth (about $230,000) to a financial adviser at one of the country's best-known companies. That young cowboy ended up putting it all in a handful of technology stocks in early 2000, which were caught in the tech wreck meltdown, reducing her nest egg by more than half in seven months. It still hadn't recovered. She was writing me to see if there was any recourse and if I could help. The answer to both questions was yes, and my representations to her broker's company yielded a fat cheque.

Having said these things, be assured that the vast majority of financial advisers in Canada are honest, reliable and very good at what they do. I work with hundreds of them from coast to coast, and am almost always impressed. But the fact remains, if you're looking for an adviser you can trust, there are some tough questions to ask. Include these:

- *What qualifications do you have?* The best one, in my view, is the CFP—Certified Financial Planner—designation. This is fast becoming a national standard, and your adviser should have achieved that or be working to do so.
- *What products or assets do you offer?* You do not want a person who just fronts for a life insurance product or mutual fund company. Your adviser should be able to offer every conceivable product, and he should be independent. If the first thing he wants to do is sell off your no-load bank mutual fund, you'd better ask why. Unfortunately, a growing trend in the business is for financial advisory companies to be creating and selling their own mutual funds. Some are fine; others are canines. Always ask precisely why a certain fund or fund family is being recommended to you.
- *How do you get paid?* There are advisers you can hire to draft a financial plan for you for a fee, but the thing still needs to be implemented. Therefore, I think for most people the best bet is an adviser who is compensated by the companies whose products you buy. Some cynics worry that a commission-driven adviser will put you into inappropriate assets, but with recent changes in the mutual funds industry, that hardly ever happens.
- *How often am I going to see you?* A good adviser will, of course, be available to take every phone call you place to her. She should also meet with you whenever you want, and make a point of reviewing your portfolio at least annually. You should get monthly or quarterly statements, or have the ability to check your holdings at any time on-line.
- *Can I see a sample plan? Or some references?* A good adviser will draft a comprehensive plan for you—some are up to twenty pages in length—prior to any assets being purchased or other actions taken. Ask to see a sample plan,

along with the names and phone numbers of existing clients whom you can call for an assessment. And make sure you follow through. Actually call the references and ask probing questions about whether the adviser has increased their wealth or peace of mind.
- *How will you deal with the big picture?* You're not seeking an adviser simply to tell you what mutual funds to hold. You need integrated and comprehensive advice on investments, tax planning, life insurance, real estate, estate planning and every other aspect of your financial life.
- *Will you give me an assessment of my situation? For free?* A good adviser will not be afraid to offer you one or two free consultations to determine the facts about your investment portfolio, tax status, hopes and goals. Based on that information, he or she will get back to you with a draft plan of action and a candid opinion of whether you are on the right path or the wrong path. An adviser who will not do this, or who sends an assistant out to interview you, is the wrong person.

Seek this kind of person out. Ask the tough questions. Be probing and realistic. And do it now. If you are having trouble finding an adviser, you can always ask me for a name or two of someone in your area. I'm always with you, at **garth.ca**.

garth.ca

Take another five minutes and go on-line to **garth.ca**. I'm a huge believer in the Internet and its ability to contain, organize and present information. This is a medium that will turn out to be more powerful than radio, television and the telephone combined. In fact, over time, it will come to absorb those technologies, causing nothing short of a revolution in human communication.

At **garth.ca** you will find daily updates on the markets and personal finance strategies, and a large, searchable base of archived information. There is also a live video feed direct from the broadcast centre of Millennium Media Television, the company of which I am chief executive officer.

Other features of special interest to readers of this book:

A weekly update

Every Sunday there is an update to this book published on-line at **garth.ca**, in the "columns" area. Please take five minutes on Sunday evening or during the week to read it. This is material I personally research and write, and it is yours to benefit from, free of charge.

A video version

Watch a video version of this book on-line. If you have been unable to attend one of my live seminars, or would like to view the latest update, here is an opportunity. The video can be watched in streaming media, downloaded or ordered—burned on a CD or in VHS format for a small charge.

The Turner Report

Ten times a year I produce an in-depth newsletter, published on the fifteenth of the month, featuring mutual fund picks, stocks to watch, tax and investment strategies, and a national panel of top financial advisers who provide complete answers to subscribers' questions. Delivered by letter mail or e-mail, *The Turner Report* is available for a small monthly fee and offers a 100% money-back guarantee. You will find more information and a free sample on-line.

If you need to reach me, here's how:

By mail:
Garth Turner
372 Bay Street, Suite 600
Toronto, Ontario M5H 2W9
Fax: (416) 489-2189

To book a seminar:
Gisele Robert
Speaker Solutions
(416) 489-2188
1-877-489-2188 toll-free

On-line: (personal) garth@garth.ca
(corporate) garth@MillenniumMedia.tv

Index

active investors, 113–114, 115
ageing population, 38, 56–59
alimony payments, 82
American dollar, adoption of, 116–120
analysts, 92
art as investment, 49
asset allocation, 97–98
asset swap, 99–100

Baby Boom generation, 27, 56–59, 102
bad stock purchases, 86
bear market, 63
Berg, Andrew, 118
big houses, 102–103
biotechnology, 22–23, 27
bonds
  capital gains, 61
  fixed-income trading, 62
  government, 60–61, 62
  income from, 63
  index funds, 62–63
  and interest rates, 61
  long *vs.* short, 61–62
  security of, 61, 62
  yield to maturity, 61
Boomernomics (Sterling), 58
Borensztein, Eduardo, 118
bull market, 63
Business Cycles (Schumpeter), 66
business insurance, 72
"buy high and sell low," 19–20

Canada Customs and Revenue Agency, 98, 112
Canada Education Savings Grant, 81
Canada Savings Bonds, 60–61
Canadian dollar, 116–120
capital gains
  elimination of taxes, potential, 107
  inclusion rate, 53, 105–106
  lower income brackets, 107
  lower-income spouse, 68
  marginal rate, 107
  wealth creation, 106
capitalism, 106
cars, 77–79
cash flow, 77–78
central bank gold lending, 30
Certified Financial Planner designation, 122
child support payments, 82

children, 80–82
Chilton, David, 59
clone technology, 22–23
common shares, 95
contributions in kind, 51–52
CPP benefits, 68
creditors, 116
cycles, 24–27

deflation, 64–67
demographics, 27, 37–38, 56–59
digital wealth, 31
diversification, 47, 59, 86–90, 92–93, 95–96
dollar-cost averaging, 59
dollarization, 116–120

education, 80–82
electronic assets, 76–77
entrepreneurs, 93
equity in home, 79, 100–101, 101–105
equity investments, 94–98
exit tax, 120

family sizes, changes in, 37–38
Finactive survey, 72–73
financial advisers, 120–123
fixed-income trading, 62

garth.ca, 124–125
gene technology, 22–23
Glenn, Jerome, 22
gold, 28–32
good debt, 101–105
Gordon, Theodore, 22
government surpluses, 39, 58
Greenspan, Alan, 67
growth investors, 113–114

harmonization of national policies, 15
Harris, Lawren, 49
HELOC. *See* home equity loan
Home Buyers' Plan, 105
home equity loan, 100–101, 101–105
home ownership. *See* real estate
house insurance, 72

income gap, 93
income splitting, 67–68
index funds
  bonds, 62–63

mutual funds, 88, 97
indexing, 114–115
inflation
  and central bank policies, 67
  core rate, 67
  defeating, 67
  inflation-deflation cycle, 65–66
  and real estate market, 38–39, 103
  self-reinforcing economic condition, 64–65
information technology, 23
inheritances, 57
insurance, 71–75
interest, deductibility of, 99, 103, 112
interest income, 55
interest rates
  and bonds, 61
  mortgage rates, 79
Internet
  access, 23
  Canadian usage, 20
  fast spread, 25
  information pipeline, 45
  technology, 20
  "upwave," 27
investing style, 8–11, 113–116
investment fund. *See* mutual funds
investment mistakes, 83

Japanese economy, 66
jewellery as investment, 75–76

"Know Your Client," 84
Kondratieff Wave, 24–27

leasing *vs.* buying, 77–79
life expectancy, 57, 70
life insurance, 72–73
location, 34–35
long-term investments, 47
Long Wave theory, 24–27

managed money, 110–111
marital breakdown, 82
market. *See* stock market
market-makers, 46
marriage, 67–68
Martin, Paul, 105–106, 107–108
"MatchMaker," 8
MERs (management expense ratios), 88
millionaires, 109
mortgage

  asset swap, 99–100
  home equity loan, 100–101
  insurance, 72
  pre-approval, 40
  rates, 79
  RRSP, 101
  strategy, 79
  tax-deductible, 98–101
mutual funds
  actively managed, 88
  costs, 88–89
  deferred sales charge, 88–89
  definition, 87
  index funds, 88, 97
  load funds, 88
  risk, 88–89
  sales commission, 88
  selling units of, 89
  stocks in, 87–88
  wealth creation, 110

nanotechnology, 23
net worth, 28
net worth worksheet, 10–11, 28
Nortel, 83, 90–93

online investment, 83–85
Ontario Securities Commission, 84

passive investing, 115
Payne, Charles, 45
pension income, 55
Perryman, Ray, 44–45
personal computers, 21–22
professional advisers, 95, 120–123

real estate
  advantages of, 32–36
  ageing population, 38
  agents, 35–36
  big houses, 102–103
  buying guidelines, 34–35
  changing family size, 37–38
  disadvantages of, 36–40
  equity in home, 79
  inflation, 38–39, 103
  investment strategy, 40–43
  recreational property, 41
  rental income, 43
  residential, 16
  supply and demand, 36–37
  tax-free housing, 43
  townhouses, 41
  true value, recognition of, 42
recreational property, 41

127

Registered Education Savings Plan, 80–82
Registered Retirement Savings Plans. *See* RRSPs
rental income, 43
renting *vs.* buying, 77–79
RESPs, 80–82
Riley, Susan, 117
risk
  and life expectancy, 70
  mutual funds, 88–89
  myth of, 68–71
  profile, 8–10
  short-term, 69
  true nature of, 70
Roth, John, 91, 92
Royal Bank Action Direct, 83–84
RRSPs
  best and worst types, 52
  contribution limit, 50–51
  contributions in kind, 51–52
  to finance non-sheltered investments, 54
  high-income retirees, 53–56
  Home Buyers' Plan, 105
  meltdown strategy, 53–54
  mortgage, 101
  reasons for owning, 50
  on retirement, 53–56
  rule of 72, 108
  self-directed, 52
  spousal, 67
  strategy, 54–55
  tax-sheltered growth, 50
  withdrawals, 53
Rubin, Jeff, 117
rule of 72, 108

safety, price of, 71
salary income, 55
Schumpeter, Joseph, 65–66
Schwab Canada, 83–84
segregated funds, 71
short-selling, 48
short-term investments, 48
short-term thinking, 69–70
space, 22
spousal RRSPs, 67
Sterling, William, 58
stock market

bear market, 63
beating the market, 112–116
bull market, 63
"buy high and sell low," 19–20
correction, 63
crash, 63
decline, 63
expected growth, 18–19
myths, 17–18
resilience, 12–16
truth about, 18
volatility, 44–49
winner, 94–98
stock purchase guidelines, 94–98
systematic withdrawal plan (SWP), 104

tax-free housing, 43
taxation, 110
TD Waterhouse, 83, 84
technology
  bear market, 58
  digital wealth, 31
  electronic assets, 76–77
  future of, 20–24
  investment mistakes, 24
  and productivity, 27
term insurance, 73–74, 75
terrorism, 15
Thomson, Ken, 49
townhouses, 41
Turner Report, 124–125
2015: After the Boom (Turner), 69

uncertainty, 12–16, 44–49
universal life insurance, 74–75
"upwave" periods, 25–27

value investors, 114
variable life insurance, 74
volatility, 44–49, 59, 96

Wealthy Barber (Chilton), 59
whole life insurance, 74
wireless applications, 27
Wolff, Ken, 46
women, financial advice for, 7–8

yield to maturity, 61